The
GOD
Participle

Copyright ©2014 Bruce 'Zen' Benefiel

Published by Be The Dream, LLC

ISBN-13: 978-0692343548 (Be The Dream, LLC)

ISBN-10: 0692343547

Introduction

So many questions arise as to how one will be accepted, judged or viewed for revealing private thoughts and well-intentioned notions. Sharing things that reject common understanding increases the opportunity for both intellectual and literary rejection, no matter the reality of the experiencer's story.

I've attempted to share a real-life story here, relating to the quest for truth and understanding. I was told very early in life that most people never go through a spiritual awakening, but if they do it is in the mid-40s. It certainly makes sense as that is when empty-nesters are looking for their next 'priorities' in life after child rearing. What questions do you have present in your life?

I'm hoping that at least two of those are, "Who am I?" and "Why am I here?" Perhaps the early awakening for me will offer some guidance and/or reflection that has crossed your mind, or perhaps your heart. I ask that you keep in mind that I'm just reporting and theorizing as I explore this cathartic path. I'm painfully aware of how it has changed my life with the trials and tribulations to date.

I'm also cognizant of the amazing benefits and joys this exploration of life and *self* have brought. What if you really wanted to know truth? Would you be willing to die for it, literally? Would you be willing to trust so deeply in something completely beyond your experience or understanding if/when it arrived to offer answers? Consider what it might take and how valuable that experience might be as one matures.

Many are looking for something more and don't know how or where to find it. I began my quest very young, for some reason, probably due to being orphaned at birth and told of my adoption as soon as I was able to understand the concept. I value that kind of honesty.

Whether we choose or want to believe what is placed in front of us for experience and/or observation, the truth is in the disclosure and discussion. We can imagine all kinds of things in our heads. It doesn't matter if we cannot find corroboration with others somehow, somewhere. It may not come quickly, either.

This story is about a life-changing event, details surrounding the scene and the notion of a soular revolution. I give the reader plenty of opportunity to find cracks and crevices that can distance the truth. If you've got a belief system that likes to find fault and judgment, you'll enjoy the plethora of places you can do that here. If you've got a belief system that is open for suspension, then you might find some useful nuggets.

Thank you for being here now.

Lead with Vision,

Zen Benefyl
MA, MBA

Contents

Introduction	5
Honesty is *Less* than Full Disclosure?	1
A Newly Ordered World	11
Confessions of a Teenager in Love	19
Dying to Know the Truth	27
A Little Help from Above	43
Challenges of Being Sensitive	53
Perception Beyond the Doors	61
Cosmic Conundrum Fulfilled	71
Inappropriate Choices?	81
Taking My Chances	95
A Separate Reality	103
The Messy Antic Complex	115
How About Transition?	129
Symbolically Speaking	135
The GOD Participle.... BEing	141
Soular Revolution	151
Explore Further	163
About the Author	165

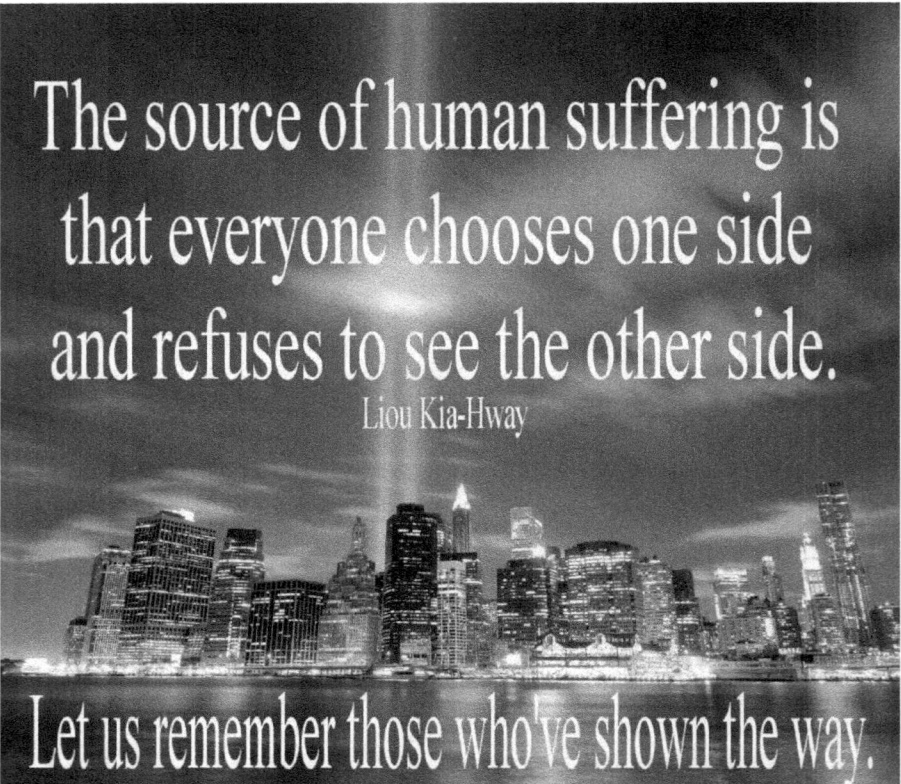

Honesty is *Less* than Full Disclosure?

Many of us have experimented with various substances in our younger years, especially in the 70s, and some may still. I'm not about to pass judgment, just acknowledgement of some realities. Psychotropics became increasingly interesting in my teens with the rise of Aldous Huxley, Timothy Leary, Ram Dass, The Beatles et al.

A voracious intellect bored with school, because of the lack of real challenge, can find release in the effects of these substances on the mind. Many students still self-medicate to get them through the days. I don't judge it or recommend it, but it is what it is. Ultimately, we still have to find the way to self-awareness clean and clear.

Carlos Castaneda was a favorite author among many and the intrigue of shamanism went beyond the dichotomy of religions so the area was ripe for exploration. Jonathan Livingston Seagull gave flight to an inquiring mind as I began to question reality deeper. None of my friends seemed that interested.

I cannot say that I am proud of my decision to explore these realms, but I certainly didn't have any brain cells destroyed in the process. I did have missed opportunities because of my choices and I'd be a liar if I said I had no regrets. Of course, I strive to free myself of them and been fairly successful.

I found that trap doors are just that. They get you in but they don't necessarily let you out. However, once you find that you can open the door it is much easier to go back and do it naturally. I'm speaking of accessing realms of consciousness of course; the 'silence' within and the realms of 'heaven.'

Frank Alper, as a newly deemed Baba Ram Dass, wrote extensively about the doorways along with Huxley, Castaneda and others. Be Here Now was one of the first books that connected the dots for me. I find it interesting that the 'spiritual' field still has major judgments on self-discovery through sacred plants or other psychotropic catalysts honored by indigenous practices. Perhaps that will change soon.

The reality was that it was only a catalyst that opened the mind to new concepts and ideologies of connectedness to ALL THAT IS. The latter being the net result, each life has to move on in the realization of it **without** the substances involved in order to live in that awareness. The door to perception opens further.

We think and act, but without the knowledge of self, and through the other side of the looking glass we have the awareness and knowledge of ourselves. It is without the substance of a separate reality, but it opens us to hearing and seeing more deeply into our own. There is no greater gift than self-reflection.

Honesty is *Less* than Full Disclosure?

I remember the first time as though it was yesterday or at least the day before. I dropped with my parents, not 'with' them but in the back seat of Dad's Buick on the way to an out-of-town high school basketball game.

I had several friends on the reserve varsity team and my parents liked supporting them too. I loved the game and would've been on the team, too, but I had literally ran over the JV coach in football practice earlier in the year and it was apparent he did not care for me after that incident. I probably would have reacted similarly, though it was hilarious when his toupee flew off in the process.

I ran a 4.3 second 40 yard dash in full gear, so I wasn't a bit sluggish off the line and I had a great sense of timing with the whistle blower that started the dash. We were doing backfield split-the-dummy hand-off exercises. As soon as we got the hand-off we had to split the large dummies in front of us, held by teammates, and go whatever direction the coach pointed after we got through the dummies.

The backfield coach sat directly on the other side and told us if he hadn't pointed by the time we got there to run him over… so I did, and embarrassed him further unintentionally. Ooops…

I was just following directions. He hadn't pointed and so, well, I did what I was told. The whole group of guys laughed as it happened. He picked himself up, along with his hairpiece that got knocked off, and proceeded to sarcastically congratulate me. Well, you can imagine the rest of the story.

I enjoyed playing defensive safety under another coach's eye and I also quarterbacked the reserve team. However, he was also the varsity reserve basketball coach. Rather than push my luck, I decided not to try out for the reserve team that year which effectively ended my basketball career.

I still played intramural ball, though, and I spent many Saturdays at the YMCA gym in Anderson playing with a lot of really good African American kids. Alexandria was bereft of any color at the time.

So there I was, launching into my first experience on 'acid.' It was pretty cool as I watched the trails from the basketball as it was being passed around and shot. I could sense that if I relaxed and let my mind go that the experience got more intense and I could sense the movement and sounds of the gym in a hypersensitive way, feeling the sounds as much as hearing them. It was curiously intriguing.

I could also bring myself back to a 'normal' state and interact with others like normal and nobody knew the difference. I even went up to one of my best friends' father and talked to him about our overnight plans for later after the game. I liked the control of being able to go in and out of the experience at will.

Some years later I went off the deep end and spoke to him and Dad about the benefits of taking LSD while they sat at our kitchen table. It was not my best choice, for sure. I only had the perspective of a teenager at the time, skewed by a sense of intrigue and potential beneficial advantages.

After we returned home and while waiting for my friend, I laid on my sister's bed (she was at a slumber party) talking on the phone to a girl and watching the patterns of headlights and shadows play on the ceiling.

The scene seemed to be breathing with me and as I looked out at the lights they were surrounded by brilliant auras of varying colors, like rainbow-sparkled bubbles undulating in the darkness.

It was drizzling rain that night too, so the refraction of the light in the rain was absolutely gorgeous. When my friend finally showed up, we went out for pizza. When he turned the windshield wipers on I remember thanking him for letting me see clearly. I couldn't help but laugh afterward. I felt so alive and bubbly in that state of being.

We both got involved in DeMolay as well. I was already a Master Councilor at the time. About a year or so later he became our Master Councilor. We had an outdoor initiation planned at a local gravel pit turned campground and swimming hole.

We had everything set up and he was to give a 'Flower Talk' to the incoming. Several of us, including the future class valedictorian, dropped just before the start of the program. Not all admit it years later, however.

Well, it started raining so we had to take everything down and move it back in town to the Masonic Temple and carry on the program there. We had planned the 'trip' to start about the time we got done with the ceremony, but it was well past the time when we finally got started.

It was his first initiation into the world of psychotropics and I knew he'd be challenged by the shift in consciousness, but he made it through the talk just fine and we returned to the campout a short time later. The rest of the evening was spent sharing perceptions and incredible thoughts about 'reality' as we explored our perceptions.

My first consciousness expansion coupled with a real visual experience came while sitting in my high school study hall, peering at the table in front of me as I had my chin resting on my hands on top of it.

As I stared at the table, I began to see layers upon layers of waveforms all nicely nestled into each other, seemingly creating the table. It was like I was seeing beyond the form.

The most vivid point was 'seeing' the layers of the laminates used in the table top. As I watched intently it appeared as though these patterns ebbed and flowed with my breath. The orchestration of their movement was truly amazing at the time. I could literally see the layers as waveforms, undulating to some magical rhythm that I could not hear....yet.

Eastern philosophy offered an explanation that everything is vibration, not near as solid as one might believe. Many years later, quantum physicists and leading-edge pioneers in the field described very similar structures to reality.

I know that was just a moment in time with a profound viewing of the nature of creation, or at least that is what it appeared like to me. Instead of just turning on, tuning in and dropping out, like Tim Leary suggested, I was intensely curious about the experience and the effects on my senses. It seemed much deeper.

I never had the 'hallucinations' that I heard about, just a much more vivid display of perceptual reality.

I got the chance to speak to Dr. Leary a couple of years before his death. My excitement waned quickly, though.

At the time Dr. Leary seemed only a shell of what I expected from one so intimately involved in the expansion of consciousness. Age and fragility takes its toll. Many years had passed and not all of them suited him. His own battle with physical reality was failing, although he still had a twinkle in his eyes.

One of my early desires had finally been fulfilled at least. I'd spoken to the man responsible for so many trips into the depths of consciousness and beyond, outside looking in as the line from the Moody Blues song proposed.

What I found later was the explanation for it all, along with a growing understanding of cooperating with the natural actions of time, space and matter. Mathematical formulas for constructing geometric shapes we all study in school really do have a connective framework with the foundational structure of time and space, thus facilitating the manifestation of matter. Recent movies like *The Matrix, What the Bleep Do We Know?, and TRON-The Legacy* hint of it.

Many years later I would return to the quest of understanding, only with my mind free of substance and much better prepared to ask prudent questions.

Those questions helped to formulate an understanding of the depths of consciousness that included similar layers that I'd seen so many years prior. I felt I was making progress.

Sitting in an advanced geometry class in high school, I became aware that many of the internal images and patterns I was seeing were indeed mathematical models of these equations, passed down through discovery and revelation of earlier inquisitors of the nature of matter. I couldn't understand what it all meant then.

All I knew was that, with eyes closed, I was seeing these same patterns in the movements of my mind and the traveling of my thoughts during those earlier experiences. I had an intuitive understanding that this was 'sacred' geometry. Many years later it became even more obvious as I studied the Fibonacci sequence and Golden Mean as natural constructs throughout reality.

Many artists and computer animation wizards are creating the same images for mandalas, wormhole effects for movies, and the imagery of the inner journey expressed on canvas. I'm still in the quest of how it flows together; to understand its significance in the natural order of our evolution, which this exploration seems to precipitate.

We are given many indicators as to how to find truth, a cohesive reality of connected experiences, in spite of what the neighbors might think. Back then there was little information to explore beyond religious texts.

Now there is a plethora of paths one can take through any chain bookstore, across the sections of occult, psychology, religion, self-help or spirituality. I found a much more exciting world within than many were able to reach, hearing and seeing more subtle realms than most people considered at the time. I found things, for a moment, at least.

There is still something to be said of the pure path, free of substance. It takes more discipline and the practice is replete with inherent benefits always, not just during a few moments of clarity.

A Newly Ordered World

I was in a new world that few even knew about, let alone could express with any surety. Something in here made sense at the core of my being, but bringing it forth into conversation was nearly impossible given the immensity of the sensations.

The OBEs of my younger years sort of prepared me for the intense inner journeys as I'd been able to go beyond the fear of death, which released me to travel down the rabbit hole to a whole new world of inner imagery as I explored further. Bob Monroe was just getting started at the time with his scientific studies and Dr. Moody had just hit the newsstands.

Of course I was just awed by the inner trips down the wormholes and through the geometrically crafted doorways into worlds of wonder. The imagery was so beautiful and flowed from one image to another with effortless transitions. Many years later I would recognize many of the same images in fractals and sacred geometry studies.

Regardless of what one might think, the internal worlds are real no matter how you might reach them. We often are fearful of entering them for some reason, though. We can't get quiet enough.

I hadn't done a lot of research on spiritual platforms yet, but this sure introduced me to the concept of what 'cosmic consciousness' might entail. I also enjoyed the conversations that deep thoughts evoked in my circle of friends, considering the possibilities of how the world could change if only people realized they didn't have to be so scared.

Now I have to say that I wasn't entirely single-minded in my approach to experiencing the inner realms on my own. I went to my share of concerts and parties, but I preferred to hang out with others that had a more intellectual to the experience rather than the 'party heartier' types.

I preferred to think more than less and engage deep philosophical questions while enjoying the opportunity to experience. One of the effects I most enjoyed was that 'serious' [drama trauma] matters became so trivial and even humorous, especially when it involved obvious ploys of the ego. It didn't bode well with others then.

It was the beginning of understanding, for me, of how utterly silly it is to believe the mind is the master, without connection to everything around us. I came to realize that the mental constraints, emotional blocks and false belief systems one carries come up for examination in so many ways in this altered state.

One truly has the opportunity to 'free the mind,' as Morpheus would say.

A Newly Ordered World

The more attached people were to stressful situations or dis-eased thoughts, their demons would rise out of the darkness of their minds to visit them in the reality of their trip. Some could handle them, some could not. My cousin found out the hard way.

After a bad trip he was put in the psyche ward and in the medical profession's infinite wisdom, was given 51 shock treatments over a few weeks' time. How insane! They left him nearly incapable of carrying on an intelligent conversation. He was a brilliant student before those events and we had some wild discussions.

I removed myself from the psychotropic scene a long time ago, but I have to say it helped me to 'free my mind' of the constraints of limited thinking early on; remaining out-of-the-box for the rest of my life. I must have a strong constitution or maybe a powerful guardian angel, but I am fortunate to have a strong mind and contemplative spirit to this day. It's all good.

I am concerned about how the youth of today try to find solace in various synthetic ways, few of them anywhere close to being healthy for the mind, body and spirit. Still, they recognize the world as it is has little to offer one who truly desires to seek the mysteries of creation's natural order. Our society is steeped in separative notions.

I tend to look at my immediate environment and extrapolate the cosmic significance in order to understand the bigger picture of how people play (or not) and what it really means to create harmony among people. I do believe that is what we truly desire… to love and be loved produces harmony.

People often say they want balance and harmony, but how they show up in life simply prohibits it and they tend to blame everyone around them instead of looking in the mirror. I got a harsh look in the mirror that offered still deeper levels of an old pattern I uncovered a decade ago. I've been working through it and am still challenged.

Changing beliefs is easy, or so we think. Somehow, though, my nemesis showed up once again… "I have a lot to offer, but you will reject me." Do you have something like that rolling around in your head and/or heart? I know where it came from – being orphaned. It shouldn't matter now as an adult, but energetically it has to be cleared from my mental/emotional world.

As an adoptee I found my search for depth in life was far more important than anything else. It still is and I'm not triggered by behaviors of others, but so many are still. The first sign is when others project their opinions like, "You think you are better than…" It sucks when people do that and nothing anyone can say will change that belief. It's locked and loaded with no concept of real truth.

The whole concept of feeling like one needs to help others to heal usually comes from a deeply wounded individual that hasn't found their own healing yet. The old adage of 'we teach what we need to learn' certainly applies if we are listening. It takes deep listening or gazing in the mirror to see yourself in that way. Try looking into your eyes in the mirror.

Most folks tend to reject that view and act out aggressively. It's sad to see it happen, even heart-wrenching when you are in the middle of it. It's even more disappointing when you've made every attempt to be the change you with to see and it just ain't happenin' around you.

So how do we show up?

Are we really authentic or do we have layers and layers of masks that we use to hide from the truth?

Do we honor others or usurp their power for our own purpose and steal their energy and resources with no respect offered?

Do we give with no expectation of return or do we play the invisible reach around that is obvious to others but oblivious to our own sight?

Do we play the victim card or do we acknowledge the choice we made to be out of integrity?

We all have our agendas and reasons for behaving certain ways. I certainly stepped out of bounds and held back in expressing my own needs in order to fulfill the needs of another. Sometimes that is the best and most gracious way to be in life. I still wonder about the boundaries.

There is a balance, a harmony of self and others that we often find challenging. We rarely communicate our true feelings, let alone ask for feedback from others about how we appear to show up in our relationships.

If we are unable to do that in our personal relationships, those that are closest and most sacred, then how can we expect to show up in a professional environment any differently? I think it was T. Harv Eker that said, "What you do anywhere, you do everywhere." Ponder that one.

I think about that a lot. I observe even more.

I review my authenticity, my intentions and my reflections as though my life depends on it. If I show up anywhere out of sync, then I probably show up everywhere out of sync. What do you think about that for your own life?

There is a lot of discussion about being able to anticipate the needs of our future business, social and technological needs. Analyzing trends is big business, but it still relies on historical values… past events. Yes, it is recent past in our current trending reviews, but still the past nonetheless.

It is my opinion that, looking through new eyes with the review of how we show up and the reflections we get, we have an obligation to create a future that is harvesting the past while engaging a rapid growth cycle. That growth comes from authentic and effective communication at all levels of our lives. That is how we can "Be the change we wish to see."

> The purpose of each soul's sojourn on earth is to learn to see beyond the evanescence of phenomena to the Eternal Reality.
>
> Paramahansa Yogananda

If I know that love is myself and that pain is also myself, that understanding is myself and suffering too, then I will be mindful.

Thich Nhat Hanh

Confessions of a Teenager in Love

Returning to the storyline, I must confess that my home life was fairly ideal with parents who really cared about my well-being and happiness. Nearly everyone in town knew them and whether I knew it or not, my activities always got back to them. I was quite popular in school, got good grades, never saw a reason to ditch, and played varsity sports from my freshman year on.

I'd met a girl as a sophomore that I fell for right away, and she for me.

It was one of those 'when our eyes met' kinda things; reciprocal attraction. She was a cheerleader as well. I began visiting her at home as her parents would not allow her out on a date yet. She wasn't from the best of homes and lived in what was considered to be 'the other side of the tracks' neighborhood. I didn't care. She was sweet, pretty and intelligent.

We went everywhere together. She was a cheerleader, too. I would pick her up before each game and even when I wasn't playing, during basketball season, I still made sure she got to the games and home again. Of course, the ride home usually took a bit longer than normal. It is amazing what you can do in an Opel GT.

We were a couple all the way through high school, virtually inseparable. Her parents thought the world of me and I enjoyed them, although they were much different than my own. Their home was small and appeared that it had many add-ons over the years.

I'm quite sure I lost focus after my senior year, feeling the angst of my future considerations. I think I just wanted freedom and used the excuse to 'break up' with her, thinking she would be there when I returned if there wasn't any action on campus.

I was so wrong. Regardless, I risked the loss over my sense of integrity thinking she would not willingly give me permission to explore other attractions at Ball State.

My own values were such that I couldn't violate her trust, yet I did. I'm sure I'm not the only guy that has made such blunders and maybe there are some who didn't risk the loss and still managed to enjoy some encounters without commitment.

Many, many years later on our way to play golf, my mother confided in me that she wasn't sure that humans were made for monogamy. We had been talking about my girlfriends over the years, since my divorce, and that I had nearly always felt something was 'missing' in my relationships.

Mom's comment was a huge shock, especially coming from one that I held so precious in the category of pristine relationships. She and dad had been together over 50 years at the time and never ever, even under intense questioning, gave any hint of violating their own relationship in any way. I was dumbfounded that she would say such a thing. Turns out it was the onset of dementia.

But, you know, I think she could be right. Pair bonding is quite rare in the animal kingdom. The idea of past lives and soul mates sure gives reasonable cause for why one might encounter such deep feelings outside a primary relationship.

What if we could freely care about others, including having sexual relations, and not feel guilt?

What if our belief systems have kept us from a greater experience of loving and being loved?

Is it so wrong to love many?

What about the soul's progression according to many mystery schools?

Is there a greater reality yet to be discovered in fullness by losing a perceived 'moral' code?

Are we really capable of loving others without attachments to their behavior?

The question is: can they love each other?

Honestly, I think our culture is not equipped for such a leap in unconditional love to step away from the conditional pair-bonding propagated by millennia of religious and social practice in the West. Perhaps we are incapable of that level of love for one another.

Circling back from that tangent in order to continue, I'd graduated 10th in my class of 300+ and was preparing to enter the pre-med program at Ball State University, having just turned 18. In the process I tested out of 5 quarters through the College Level Examination Program, so I started as a 6th quarter sophomore. I did amazingly well on the tests, but it still didn't dawn on me that I might actually be brilliant, let alone a genius.

This was my first time living away from home, even though Muncie and Ball State were only a half-hour away. I was living in the honors dorm on the north side of campus, Swinford Hall, on the top floor of four and had a roommate from Terre Haute named Eric. It was his second year. He introduced me to much of the campus life, but he was not as gregarious so he left out a few necessary details.

I didn't try out for sports, but I did join a flag football league with a bunch of guys from our floor. We were called the 'Off Brothers.' I found out later that the name had to do with getting really stoned before games. Evidently it was a tradition. We still seemed to do quite well most of the time. At worst, we had a great time.

I had a full academic load, 17 credit hours, and managed to make it through the first quarter with a 3.33 average. My first quarter's academic effort was pretty darn good, considering I still hadn't developed any real study habits from high school and I was smoking pot on a regular basis. I just read the books, did the work when necessary and showed up in class. In spite of my pseudo-success academically, I was missing someone.

There had been no 'hook ups' with attractive young college coeds and I missed the connection I shared with my high school sweetheart. It grew stronger as time passed. I really missed the feeling I had with her and thought I better do something about it.

I returned home with the intent of asking my high school beau to marry me. Like I said before, I had 'broken up' with her because I didn't want to violate my integrity (in my own mind) in case I met or was approached by another girl at school. Yeah, well, teenagers don't have a lot of wisdom you know. At that time I was full of myself and dreamed of many encounters happening in the new environment and freedom from home. But I had no game. I was shy.

In any case, after I dropped off laundry at home I went to her house - full of anxiety, excitement and trepidation. I wasn't sure how she would receive me. I knocked on the door and her father answered. I asked if she was home and he replied, "Haven't you heard?"

My heart leapt into my throat. "Heard what?" I asked, thinking she'd been in an accident or had been mortally wounded. I came to find out that she was already married... a few weeks before.

I was heart-broken, bereft of feeling in the moment. I thought I'd made the right decision, only I didn't think about the consequences before I made the choice. Funny how we often do that in life.

Remember, teenagers don't have a lot of emotional wisdom yet. They barely have started to ask the right questions to get it, let alone have any emotional intelligence beyond self-interests.

I returned home disappointed, depressed and heart-broken. I felt lost and alone and even though my parents were shocked that she was married already, they could only offer encouragement of life moving on somehow. Yeah, they could say that. They met as grade schoolers, maintained a friendship all through school, got married and never had to face the separation from a lover.

Confessions of a Teenager in Love

I have to say they were a poor example for a child to learn about reality; the pain and suffering of love. They were together for 61 years of marriage, a bit frail and delirious at times, but still very much in love. Dad is gone now and Mom's dementia causes her to relive his passing often. I can only imagine how horrible that must be.

Actually they were the best example that one could have to learn about relationships, working through any difficulty and remaining true to their values. I never witnessed them argue, but they revealed later in life that they had their fair share. Still, conversations were always open as far as I could tell. They taught me that honesty and openness were prerequisites for happiness.

Through meditation, we practice resurrection in every moment. This is the practice of living in the everyday. We must not lose ourselves in the past or in the future.

Thich Nhat Hanh

Follow the stream, have faith in its course. It will go its own way, meandering here, trickling there. It will find the grooves, the cracks, the crevices. Just follow it. Never let it out of your sight. It will take you.

Sheng-Yen

Dying to Know the Truth

I returned to school with my whole life ahead of me, but feeling like I had nothing to live for now. I went inside and withdrew into my emotional quagmire. I was silent for a time, even in the classroom, where I'm usually quite outspoken and provocative. I hurt deep inside; a gaping hole in my heart I wasn't sure how to fill or even if I could with human love.

So, one evening I knelt in prayer. "Heavenly Father, I want to know truth, eternal truth, and I'm willing to die for it if necessary."

Although short, this heart-felt cry was a most intense prayer from my heart. I called out from the depths of the despair within me to seek something totally beyond me now. I don't really know if many go through this, especially at that age. Strange as that may seem, the outer world has a profound effect on the development of the inner connections, or lack of them, due to the struggles involved and how we choose to handle them.

The following week after school one day I was listening to the debut album of a band called 'Journey,' lounging on my dorm room bed in a pseudo-meditative state. The album itself was a testament to the journey of self and the style of the music was much different than traditional rock-n-roll. It was an invitation to explore.

Their music took one from the depths of tumultuousness to the heights of heaven, soaring like an eagle in the ethers of consciousness.

As I listened I fell into the deep depression of being alone and wondered how I would ever recover. I became silent in that feeling. During the second song on the album, ***In the Morning Day***, there was a pause after the lyrics before the vamp played out. What came next has affected my spiritual path and daily life since.

Out of nowhere I heard that familiar 'Voice' say, "Bruce, are you willing to die for what you believe in?" Immediately the 'Voice' had my attention and I thought for a moment about what I believed in strongly enough to give up my life. I felt like I was put on call, above all calls, and my mind careened as I searched for the answer. I thought, 'Jesus Christ,' but more - 'Christ Consciousness' was the fullness of what I was ready to accept as the call.

I thought it was the clearest path, but it wasn't quite 'complete' within me. The thought of Cosmic Consciousness came to mind and with that I felt it 'safe' to move forward.

Just as I said, "Yes," to the question the music continued with a guitar riff that sounded sort of like a jet going by at Mach 3. The timing was so perfectly exquisite. I felt myself gently drifting upward, away of my body and so I let go and followed the movement.

I turned and looked back to see my body lying across my bed, my head leaning against the wall and my pillow and my feet on the floor.

When I turned back to look where I was going I was immediately and totally engulfed in white light... feeling at one with God. It felt like home; warm, effervescent and serene, resting in the energy of unimaginable pure love.

I could see, but only white light. I could think, so I knew I was conscious. I had no tactile sensations of having my body, though. There was no element of fear whatsoever, only the pure feeling of this total surrender to love – completely free of any judgment. I did not 'see' any personage or anything else for that matter.

I was aware that I could think, hear, and see, so I knew that I was still very much 'alive' even in this new place that I'd only heard you go to when you die. I had totally let go of any attachment to life, but felt like I was more alive than I had ever known, humming like an amazingly powerful electric field. Talk about having a buzz…

It felt like I was wide-open in this field, yet silent and alone in the light as there was no 'voice' now.

The paradox was that I felt connected to everything and everyone, I felt a 'oneness' of being. Only years later did I understand that oneness in a more explicable way.

Still, as an impetuous teen that bored easily and thrived on exploration of consciousness, I asked, "Is there more?" I felt another slight movement and found myself in the center of a sphere of pinpoints of light with an indigo background. The blue-blackness made the points stand out significantly in stark contrast.

I gazed in complete awe as I recognized what I've heard called 'nirvana' in Eastern texts. Wow!

It seemed like I could have counted the points of light had I so desired, as there were only a few hundred or so readily visible in this place of space. I could see in any direction I wanted simultaneously with a simple thought and without sensing any movement. They all seemed to be of the same intensity, but I could tell there was a depth of field in this celestial scenery.

As I pondered these points of light, I instinctively and intuitively recognized that they were points of consciousness, whether in body or not I wasn't sure. I knew I sure wasn't at that time. Just as I made the completion of this recognition the 'Voice' resumed.

"These are those that you are to work with in order to facilitate the new world order. It will happen in your lifetime. Know this to be true. Your path will be full of trials and tribulations. Trust and have faith that everything you need will be there at the appointed time. Trust and allow."

As I heard the finish of these words I felt another rush of energy. It was stronger than the other two movements. It felt like when I used to snap back into my body from an OBE, only as soon as I felt the 'landing' I immediately took a big gasp of air, like I had actually not been breathing for those moments. It was such a sacred breath.

I kept my eyes closed for a few moments, totally enjoying the reintegration process as my body felt oh, so wonderful to me. I noticed my breathing in a way that I never had before, like a gift. The feeling of being 'born again' was as great as the feeling in the white light had been. I eventually opened my eyes and wondered what the *f..* had just happened to me. I didn't want to more for quite a while.

I could only relate to the experience as it was – with everything that happened as REALITY – because it was my direct experience. I heard years later that in most philosophical and psychological schools of thought, perception is reality.

Knowing much more about how music and lyrics can subliminally affect one's experience, it was no surprise when I went back and discovered the lyrics again. I can't tell you how many times I had listened to the album already before the experience and even sung along without really understanding the lyrics.

I'd even memorized the lyrics so I could sing along. I think most of us have particular music that affects us profoundly. I agree with those who feel music is the language of the soul, often profound and prophetic in its effects. Indeed, this album affected me more than I realized.

Just check out what the lyrics of the first two songs on the album:

Of a Lifetime

The mist is slowly lifting
The sound of life misplaced your mind
You're sitting, spellbound thru out time
I hope that you remember what you find
Singin' 'bout a lifetime

You put it down-all that I'm thinking
but take a long and distant search, when all is right you take for granted
You can't look down but you're no worse.
Singin' 'bout of a lifetime, yeah

The countless visions that are drifting
The silver dreams you hate to lose.
There's no harm, we've all been waiting.
Well keep your faith. Do what you choose.
Singin' 'bout of a lifetime

In the Morning Day

Everybody's got the blues
In the morning day, yeah
If you find the answer
And you wonder
Let's find a way
I want to give you happiness
Just like the sun gives to the day
I'd like to make you mine yeah
I'm gonna make you mine
Just like a blinding dream
Yeah, you're gonna be with me
Strolling through a summer's breeze,
And you find it's not the rain,
Leaving wrong behind you,
All your fantasies so very plain.
I want to give you happiness
Just like the sun gives to the day
I'd like to make you mine, yeah
I'm gonna make you mine
Just like a blinding dream
Yeah, you're gonna be with me.

Closer examination revealed just how influenced I was, but the intent was pure and righteous. My mind became the insatiably curious one again, so I immediately went to the campus library in search of empirical data... or something in writing that explained what I had just went through.

I knew there had to be *something* but wasn't sure I'd find anything.

In 1975 there was not much information available at the time. Even though I knew internally, in those depths of understanding beyond mental activity, I still needed the intellectual explanations to help me get a handle on some kind of congruent reality that I could live. I had some preparation from the books I'd been reading, but they were static.

I needed a current living explanation of what I had experienced. Even though it was so real, I need corroboration of some kind of validation. Imagining it all just wasn't part of my conclusion.

The best explanations I could find were of near-death-experiences where people had died on the operating table or in a horrific accident, only to return to their bodies after experiencing a tunnel with a light at the end, or seeing dead relatives and sometimes even seeing a spiritual figure of their religion waiting for them, sometimes speaking to them as well.

I had none of these elements in my experience. Why? I wondered. The message seemed to be beyond boundary, not specific to any religious or philosophical mindset. It was an enigma to say the least, but I *knew* it was of the highest order and purposeful intent.

Now I'd also heard the stories of Satan appearing as an angel of light and that he would use this disguise to deceive people into following him. It seemed that many Christian 'believers' held that no one could have revelatory experiences nowadays, let along talk to God personally.

There was always a mediator, an intercessor with some 'sanctioned' permission to speak. That philosophy seemed dead, uninhabitable by what I knew to be true. I had experienced oneness.

In every religion I'd studied so far there was always an intermediary and any 'direct' contact bordered on the side of 'demonic possession' in current times. Of course there were the stories of such cases where the demons had entered at the behest of Satan trying to take over their soul and wreak havoc on the unsuspecting. I've never felt that to be the case.

There was something deep inside of me that felt like there was much more to the story than anyone was willing to admit.

I never felt like I was possessed by a demon, approached by Satan or had any inclination to kill or murder or go postal on my fellow students. There was only the desire to know Truth and to live in unconditional love. The ability to harm another, reject the concept of creator-connection, claim to be a 'messenger of God' was never in my scope of vision. I just wanted to serve Truth.

All I wanted to do was connect the dots from my experience and find meaning to my life.

So the first place I went was the double volume dictionary just inside the Ball State University Library doors to look up the word 'satan' and find out what it said. The volumes were displayed on a large lectern just in front of the help desk. I thumbed through the pages until I found the entry.

To my ultimate surprise the very first dictionary reference was to the Greek 'thetan' which meant 'thinker.' My mind was instantly at ease, like it just proved something I'd known instinctively.

Of course, I thought, it only makes sense that the truth is that our mind **is** the 'deceiver' and all our battles were in the mind rather than choosing the love in our heart to guide us through any disturbance. We are just way too quick to go to the dark side, the negative thoughts and feelings of separation. There are no arguments of power in the heart-felt unity and oneness that I had just experienced. I only wished I could share it.

I told my adoptive parents about my 'revelation' a few days later and found myself speaking with a psychiatrist within the next week. I assured them I wasn't crazy but I guess I did need to talk about the experience so I could learn from it.

I told them even at that time that without a direct experience of their own it would be hard to comprehend mine. They thought I was 'on drugs' and on 'LSD' specifically.

I *almost* wish that I was on some drug because it would have made it much easier to dismiss the entire experience. I wasn't and I knew even a couple of bong hits weren't going to send me into hyperspace like that.

As an adult now, I know it would be a normal reaction from people who had no direct experience from which to relate. Of course it was due to drugs…. Riiiight.

I still find that so today whenever I share things in group settings. It's often beyond the scope of their experience even in the more open groups. People seem to be inherently skeptical at best. The event does sound quite incredulous I have to admit, but the *way* it happened was too perfect.

It took me many years to understand the dynamics of what those few moments truly meant and what my life's mission was in accordance with the experience of being in the presence of God (or whatever name is appropriate). I knew the purpose for my life. That was the easy part. I was on the way at least. Perhaps the rest would flow.

I also had to figure out just 'how' it was all going to happen and what I needed to do to facilitate the process, as I had been told I would. I figured finding out about how reality works was my first task. I was caught up in the experience, though, and not very rational about its implications.

What did it mean? Was I the One?

How was I to fulfill this mission?

Now that has been a lifelong task and as soon as I think I have an answer... another question presents. I'm constantly looking inward and reflecting on what is happening in my outer world. Sometimes I feel really connected. Other times I'm not sure of anything, but I know there are answers somewhere.

I think the vacillation of feelings and thoughts are designed to keep us questioning, going deeper into the understanding of reality as we know it.

I perceive that the explorations of our curious or inquisitive thinking also affect the reality we experience. Most recently the 'new age' world was rocked by The Secret and the Law of Attraction. The presentation of the precepts involved is ageless. As a man thinketh…so shall he BE.

Just to refresh your memory on the precepts of the Law of Attraction, let's look at the definition.

From Wikipedia:

The law of attraction is the name given to the belief that "like attracts like" and that by focusing on positive or negative thoughts, one can bring about positive or negative results. This belief is based upon the idea that people and their thoughts are both made from "pure energy", and the belief that like energy attracts like energy. One example used by a proponent of the law of attraction is that if a person opened an envelope expecting to see a bill, then the law of attraction would "confirm" those thoughts and contain a bill when opened. A person who decided to instead expect a cheque might, under the same law, find a cheque instead of a bill.

Although there are some cases where positive or negative attitudes can produce corresponding results (principally the placebo and nocebo effects), there is no scientific basis to the law of attraction.

The lack of scientific fact is often countered by the observation of how one thinks and feels strongly about a certain outcome, then moves toward it as a reciprocal action takes place in the world of matter that is initiated by the intention of the person desiring to create the event or product.

Indeed it may just be the result of using one's skillset to conceive and create a plan, then implementing it to produce the desired result. Anything is possible when specific understanding of project management techniques is applied, like an applied science of manifestation. However, it's the synchronistic circumstances and/or events that happen along the way that give credence to an 'unseen force' that apparently is responding to the intention, thoughts and feelings of the producer.

Perhaps you might relate to an event in your own life where such occurrences have happened beyond anything you could explain at the time. Chance meetings or serendipitous findings are an example. The whole concept of 'magnetizing' one's thoughtmosphere sure hedges the edge of modern science, but quantum physics and the theory of 'entanglement' (spooky action at a distance as Einstein called it) do give some indication of the potential validity within human capacity.

We certainly don't know just how powerful our minds can be yet we understand that the more we know about consciousness and thought, the possibilities of its potential reality increase. It does give one the cause for a pause in consideration.

Back to the storyline… Was my experience all in my imagination? Apparently not. Through my own intention or will I attracted an experience to fulfill my desire to know truth.

On the other hand, a religious person may say that my prayer was answered in a way that only God, or an emissary thereof, could accomplish. The Voice certainly seemed all-powerful, yet there was also a loving softness to it as well. I had so many more questions after the event and there seemed to be no one around that was willing to assist.

Sharing the experience only seemed to bring about critical views of my state of sanity, but mostly people just distanced themselves. I felt abandoned and alone in the world. I just needed to talk to someone that would listen without judgment or trying to offer some reason for my apparent break from reality in their minds.

Telling my parents didn't help either. Their response was fear-ridden, afraid their beloved son had lost his bearings with the world as they knew it. The look in their eyes was devastating. I only wanted them to listen and talk about it without the emotional trauma, but instead they made an appointment with a local psychiatrist. I have to say it was a God-send.

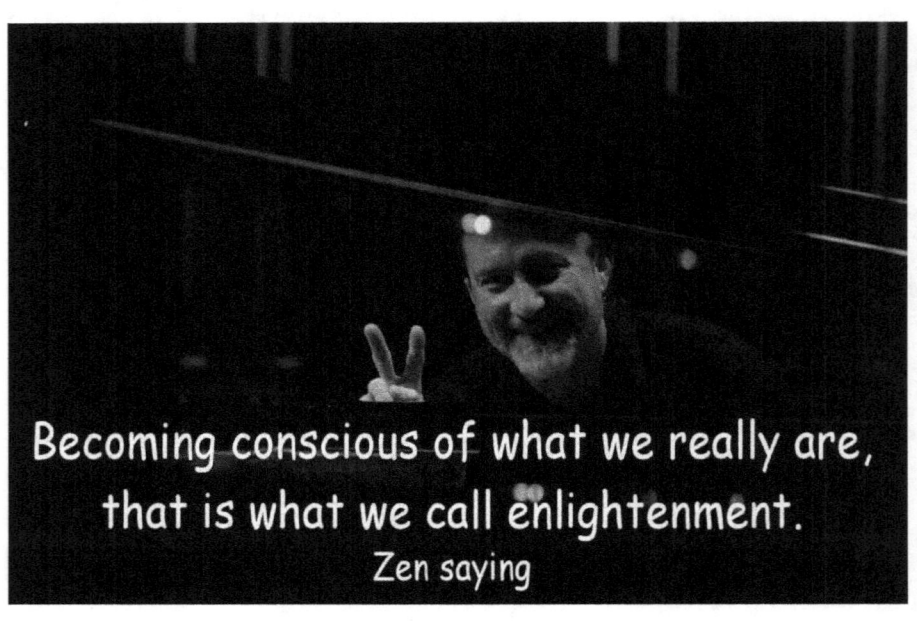

It is now – the magic of the present moment – that connects the present with the wisdom of the past.

Chogyam Trungpa

A Little Help from Above

The psychiatrist had his own perfect role in this process. Dr. Abell (quite the appropriate name - A Bell) listened intently as I described my experiences from childhood through the White Light. It took nearly three sessions to get through it all. He asked pertinent questions along the way to 'check in' with my coherence and observations of my own experience. I've always enjoyed those discussions.

I was able to distance myself from emotional obsession of its importance and reflect from an observer's perspective without a problem. Even though I could remain free of attachment, the importance or sharing wasn't always in my best interest. At least I felt like Dr. Abell was listening and he certainly wasn't telling me I was wrong or misguided. He asked deep questions.

His office was in a historic two-story in downtown Anderson, Indiana. About half way through the third session he confided in me. "Bruce," he said, "I don't think you are crazy at all. As I've listened to your experiences, it appears to me that you have all the classic signs of one going through what is known as a 'spiritual awakening.' Most people don't experience anything like this until their mid-40s, if they ever do. I'm curious as to why you are experiencing this so young."

"I think it goes without saying that it is not a good idea for you to talk so openly about it, especially with your parents, at this point in time." I heard that as meaning, 'Keep your mouth shut for now.'

He went on to share something I would have never expected from a psychiatrist. He asked me to follow him upstairs as he would like to show me something. I was about to get some confirmation that would rock my world.

I followed him up the stairs and to our right, he opened the first door. My heart nearly exploded out of my chest as the door opened. I realized some time later it was my heart chakra opening to the graciousness of the world I was about to enter.

I peered inside the door and noticed bookshelves lined with books nearly covering all the walls along with metaphysical posters and icons placed around the room. I was amazed that he could be so 'hip' and that my parents chose him. Somehow I suspected they were not aware of these 'other' methodologies in his practice.

Just inside the door at the top of the stairs was a fold up table with a deck of tarot cards setting in the center of it and two chairs on opposite sides. He asked me if I knew what the tarot cards were and I explained that I did, citing my understanding of them being tools to gain understanding through setting oneself aside and 'conferring' with the Divine Source.

He asked me if I had ever had a 'reading.' I replied that I had not. He asked if I would be interested in exploring their insights. "You need to ask," I thought. I knew I could not tell my parents about this for sure. I admitted that I would love to see what they had to offer about my experiences and life. I could use all the help.

I can only say that the reading, according to his interpretation and my acknowledgements, revealed that there was truth in what I had shared of my experience and much more to come. The reading seemed to echo what the 'Voice' had told me on the other side of the Light with expanded explanations. I felt overwhelmed.

I still was confused about what it all meant, although it was quite clear that I was in for one heck of a ride in this life. I took the red pill without realizing it. I wanted to free my mind.

Looking back on my first 'reading' it was quite apparent that my life was going to involve the quest for Truth and figuring out the means for which to share understanding, leading toward a new living awareness of harmony among people and planet.

My youthful naivety prohibited me from the wisdom I knew I needed.

Contemplating what was in store created emptiness beyond the imaginings. I had no answers. I had a litany of questions that kept growing each time I thought I found an answer.

My young mind could not even begin to wrap itself around the journey I was about to embark upon. I knew that my purpose was to find these points of light and figure out a way to collaborate with them in order to facilitate a new world order.

I knew this was to happen in my lifetime, yet it seemed like such a dream at the time. Maybe it still is. Based on my experience to date, I knew it would be a great challenge to discuss, let alone embody. It carries tremendous humility.

I kept the knowledge to myself for many years, even throughout my marriage and initial move to Phoenix, although I did manage to meet some folks in very strange ways that seemed to be somehow tuned in to my investigations. I kept the faith and enjoyed those spontaneous moments.

Over a decade later I formed a consulting company called Be The Dream to apply this 'harmony among people and planet' attitude in organizational development. I called myself a 'peace consultant' and used one of my favorite images, the pyramid

A Little Help from Above

and capstan, as my initial logo to invoke the all-seeing eye. I was idealistic to say the least.

Living that purpose has indeed made my life full of trials and tribulations. Most people never find out what their true life's purpose is, even in their 40s and beyond. Yet, at 18, I was informed. I didn't have to search for it. I just had to live it now. That is sure easier said than done.

I wasn't concerned as to what that might mean as far as my own identity, future exposure, or how I would be perceived. I did not take Dr. Abell's advice, except in rare instances, and kept sharing my contemplations and experiences throughout my life. I walk the solitary path most often.

Now that I'm older, I've had many more experiences that have led me down the path of discovery of Self and Identity. I'm amazed at how the fabric of life is so connected and I'm still a bit reluctant to accept the fullness of it, even though it appears to be true beyond any reasonable doubt.

I recently formed an events company, United We Stand Productions, LLC, to share the science and technology of how to apply what quantum physics and advanced consciousness studies are proving to be possible and that is only the beginning.

What I remain focused on is not the identity... it is THE WORK. I gave my life to know truth. Knowing it compels one to act on it, follow its lead and perform as necessary to fulfill it.

This 'mission' is still the most important aspect of my life as an adult. To facilitate a new world order based on harmony among people and planet is indeed a life-long process, complete with attending trials and tribulations. There are so many aspects of consciousness and consideration.

Even when one has a vision of a collaborative undertaking, it is imperative that there is a connection with others who can see and understand it as well, otherwise it will go nowhere. That doesn't mean I'm the leader, only that there is a collective vision and that I'm one of the facilitators.

What is even more crucial is the sharing of life-empowering and sustaining technology, both material and psychospiritual, allowing the imagineering visions of many to become as one.

As I've shared the concepts and creation of such an accomplishment, it became obvious that there needed to be a model that could both demonstrate the living awareness and provide the scientific proof of its validity.

Assimilating various pieces (everything is present and just waiting to be connected) became the foundation for a written plan. I wrote it initially for my Bachelor of Science degree in Business as my final project. I failed miserably because of the lack of related information and statistical references, but I did it. I didn't care about the grade.

Maybe it matters who I am, but it probably doesn't. It is not about 'me' in this life. If it takes standing up and being identified as anything, then it is a small price for assisting bringing some kind of harmony to this beautiful world, especially in these times of academic, environmental, political, religious, and social disorder that seems to be growing. We need to learn to get along.

Harmony is not without challenge or conflict. A good friend, the Western attorney for the new Karmapa and Aikido instructor, says that in reality there is no conflict; it is miscommunication that creates discord.

Harmony is the result of the wise use of the perceived conflict to empower communication between people to work together collaboratively.

Might I suggest that we begin to focus on socially responsible programs and environmentally sustainable living environments, including renewable energy resources?

It appears America has the opportunity to lead the way now, since we have learned the ways of corporate-sponsored and ill-advised political administration of recent years.

These concepts and ideas are nothing new to the consciousness of mankind. Learning to put down the weapons and use our arms for hugging instead is a giant leap from where we are today. Shall we go so far as to call it an Evo-Leap – an evolutionary leap in consciousness?

No ego without WE go.

Learning the TRUTH is what I've been doing since that first conversation with God, long before Neale Donald Walsh invited the world to join his conversation. It is about pure sharable energy sustained through our hearts, directed by our minds and made visible through the actions of our bodies... as natural as the movements of our solar system through the cosmos.

I respect the efforts that organized religions have made in an attempt to share righteous ideals with their congregations, but there has been something left out in my humble opinion. There is Living Word outside of the confines of the Bible or Quran or Bhagavad Gita.

It [Living Word] resides in each one of us. Every time I get into a conversation with 'Christians' who

A Little Help from Above

walk the streets proselytizing, it is the same story... they judge one as blasphemous who tries to get them out of the Book and experience the reality of the Word, the Living Word within our hearts. If they only knew....

On a practical level, there are a new set agreed upon notions known as the ISO 26000 Social Responsibility Standards. You can find them at http://planetarycitizens.net/iso-26000/

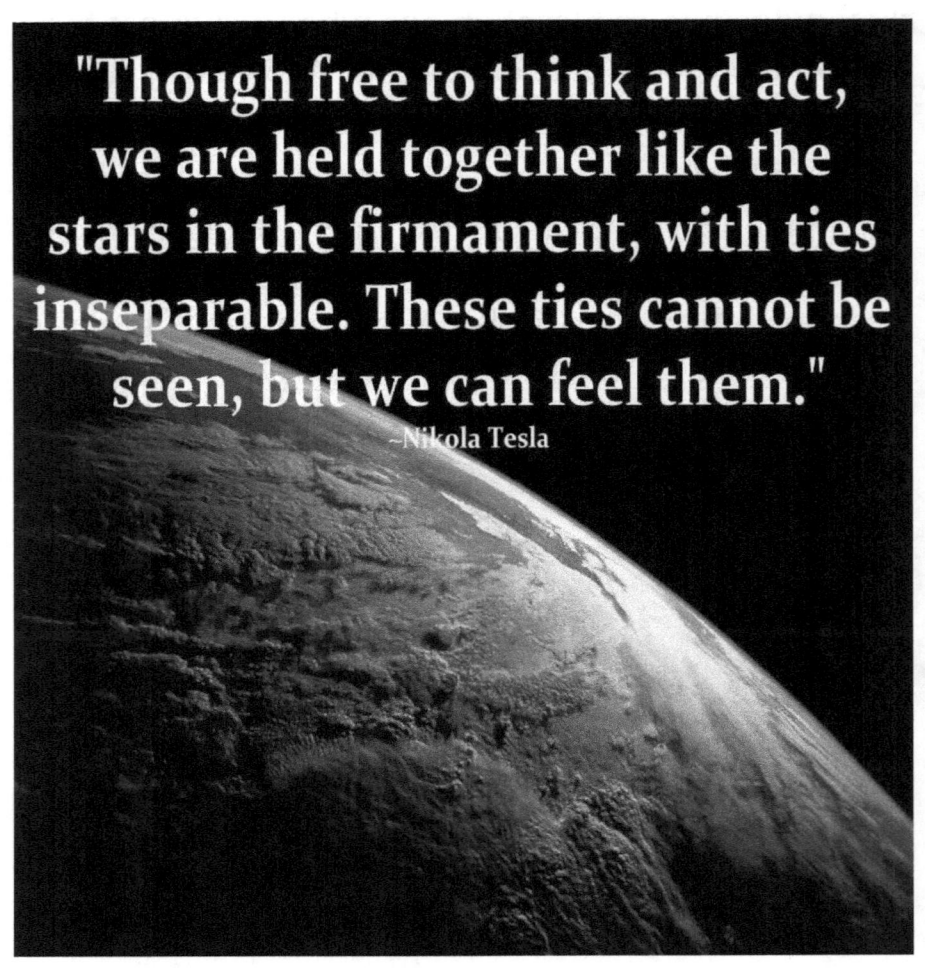

"Though free to think and act, we are held together like the stars in the firmament, with ties inseparable. These ties cannot be seen, but we can feel them."
~Nikola Tesla

Only the intelligence of love and compassion can solve all problems of life.

Krishnamurti

Challenges of Being Sensitive

During the rest of my first year, as I continued college amidst the party paradigm that most beginning students without discipline experience, I also continued my exploration into the deeper realms of consciousness. Beyond the normal studies of Biology, Chemistry, Statistics, and English, I was a voracious reader of metaphysical books and spiritual texts.

After my initial white light experience, I felt it imperative to know more about past spiritual masters and their writings and lives, even though I felt Christ to be the epitome of them all. I also began to thirst for direct experience. So now I did choose to go further into psychotropics, too.

Be Here Now, the Bhagavad Gita, Siddhartha, Doors of Perception - Heaven and Hell, The Teachings of Don Juan, and the Urantia Book were just a few of the books that I poured through at the time. I also began more astral travel, psychokinetic and telekinetic experimentation during this period. I all seemed to flow naturally.

I'd met a guy in high school who turned up in one of my classes and we became fellow explorers. Gary worked as a grounds keeper for one of the most well-known spiritualist communities in the world at the time - Camp Chesterfield.

Through our association I found that, along with a few others, we could do some amazing things. We discovered we could move energy back and forth between us as we sat across the room from each other. This energy was emanating through the palms of our hands and could be directed at will, it seemed or rather *with* will.

It took a lot of concentration to focus. Years later I read about parapsychology experiments at prestigious universities like UCLA that matched, or at least closely resembled, those things we just stumbled upon as we wondered what we could do with our minds and the energy.

Were these imaginings? I still was very much the scientist and considerate enough to check with the various students on their condition. Increased sensitivity from use of psychotropics seemed to make a big difference as well. I lived on the top floor of the honors dorm at the time and many of my dorm mates were involved in this exploration of conscious connections. It was a laboratory.

We were teenagers with too much time and curiosity on our hands. It was strange and wonderful that these experiences seemed to echo what I would learn much later about auras, energy and spiritual interconnectedness. The lack of responsibility sure helped as our minds were free to explore.

Challenges of Being Sensitive

There were other times when the empathic/telepathic experiences were a bit much to deal with for anyone. I became aware that I could hear many different voices as I traveled back and forth from the honors dorm to the cafeteria, where I worked part-time as well. It was a novelty at first, but grew to be disconcerting.

I could hear very negative remarks that seemed to be all directed at me. "You asshole, you are so stupid!" "You worthless piece of sh..!" "Can't you get it right?" "You are such a f..g idiot!" And so on... definitive 'you' as the focus... me.

After hearing all that in the space of walking a few yards outside the cafeteria one afternoon, I was so rattled and spooked that I returned to my dormitory and locked myself in my dorm room for a couple of days while I freaked out. I was paranoid for no reason, I would come to find out.

I called my friend Gary in an effort to get some kind of reality check. He and Carolyn, his girlfriend, came over and we talked it through. With their help I realized that the voices were not my own and that the comments always began with 'You...,' which allowed me to realize that I was hearing the thoughts of others and not going crazy with my own self-deprecation. Whew...!

I have to say that I did have my share of self-deprecating thoughts, but not to that extent. The voices were definitely not my own, so I had reason to release my vice-grip hold on considering possible insanity and contemplate a more global 'you' in this instance. We all talk to ourselves.

What I eventually recognized was there seemed to be a constant negative self-talk going on within the minds of students at the time, mine included. I'm sure it is consistent with students today as well, feeling like they have to be perfect in their actions and studies, beating them up internally for every little mistake.

At any rate, there were times that I would be so sensitive to these 'voices' that I thought they were focused on me. In research and study many years later I found the patterns of perdition were prolific in society, prohibiting personal growth and creating unnecessary separation in reality.

Only as I began to *observe* when they would happen did I realize they were coming from the other students as we would pass on the walkways on campus. Thank God I had someone that I could talk to that helped me to see clearly.

When the experiences first started happening, though, I had to figure out what these voices were in my head and why they were so negatively oriented.

Challenges of Being Sensitive

I learned later that took a tremendous amount of courage, but that embracing them led to freedom.

I became less affected by them as I realized that they were outside of me rather than coming from within. Still, it was a tough time for anyone going through 'sensitivity training' and admittedly I had some of those thoughts, too. Knowing that really helped me when I taught 'special ed' high school kids much later. It allowed me to really connect with them and help them discover their strengths.

Apparently with the lack of distractions and responsibilities of life, our awareness is able to advance without much disciplined practice. Baba Ram Das' *Be Here Now* really made a lot of sense. LSD allowed Westerners to experience Eastern spiritual realms without the disciplined mediation practice. I felt like the information spoke of truth and I trusted it, for then.

Experiencing the freedom that resulted from allowing this innate 'trust' to permeate our lives gave us opportunity beyond imagination. One of the things I really enjoyed were the times that Gary and I would consciously get out of our bodies and go exploring around the campus together. My old OBE training made it easy in altered states. I didn't have to wait until I was relaxed and ready for bed.

It was amazing! We could actually 'see' each other as we exited our bodies. We stayed around the dorm most of the time, as we hadn't realized at that point that we could travel further, much like my younger days. The notion of seeing each other with different eyes kept us focused on the nearness of things.

Instead, we would observe the activity in the lounge area connecting the women's and men's honors dorms. The honors dorm was actually in a V shape with a female and male wing, connected by a common lobby area with couches, a couple of TVs, two pool tables, a tabletop shuffleboard and a grand piano. There were a few small tables as well, mostly used for card or board games.

Several times we were able to observe others in the lounge, re-enter our bodies and return to the lounge and relate what they had been doing. Not too many people were real excited about the fact we could do this. In fact, it was a bit scary to most of them as they were unable to comprehend that we all have these abilities. Sound familiar?

Rarely did we find our experiments to meet with acceptance at first. The Midwest is fairly conservative and steeped in Christianity of organized religion fame... fearing and judging everything that appears outside the realm of experience and/or understanding.

Challenges of Being Sensitive

Music was also a great facilitator of these internal and external 'bridge' experiences as well. I already knew that music was supposed to be the language of the soul. What I didn't realize was that it seemed the progression of music was such that it held many keys to the discovery of my own identity and the understanding of many emotions related through musical expression. Journey, the Moody Blues, Rush and Yes were big favorites at that time... still are to this day.

Many personal fears can be addressed during the process of listening to music and the deeper one goes into consciousness, the more clearly one can see their connection to the cosmic cords woven throughout the music.

Now, this also brings up the question that is often raised about the ONE who is the Angel of Light and Music, Lucifer. Eckankar[1] is a practice based on the study of Light and Sound.

Eckankar offers its practitioners a way to examine their spiritual body and learn how to travel with it through the ethers using the 'sound current.' It's been proven that vibrational waves are what truly

---

[1] a Westernized version of the Punjabi Sant Mat or Radha Soami Satsang spiritual tradition. ECKANKAR was founded in 1965 by Paul Twitchell (c. 1908–71).

make up our physical reality. This kinda slaps modern day Christianity in the face... rather rudely I might add. *Google: Multi-Plane Awareness*.

The fear, guilt and shame scenarios are losing their grip on the congregation. I had to attend to yet another rite of passage as I was not one to keep my mouth shut, nor was I without very creative actions in time of need.

Perception Beyond the Doors

One of the more subtle realizations, quite profound in its comprehension, was a particular night I recall where I was able to sense the energy of people inside their dorm rooms. That may sound a bit bizarre, yet the experience was quite disconcerting at first, to say the least, as it was also profound.

At times of particular sensitivity and while in an altered state, I could literally 'feel' the energy of other students as I passed their rooms in the dormitories. I already had that sense in close proximity of others, but this was even broader in scope, let alone experience.

If no one was in the room it felt cold and empty, almost like an abyss could easily suck me in. On the other hand, if there was someone in the room I could feel a warm glow emanating from the room. If they were in an altered state, some I knew meditated; I could feel a gentle push from their energy, like a thick pillow being gently placed on my skin.

Now if they were engaged in any kind of psychotropic I was literally pushed up against the opposite wall in the hallway. I was so loose or rather 'empty' as I walked that sometimes it felt like I was nearly being thrown against the opposite side of the hallway. I was never afraid of this experience at all.

I had a sense of the magic and mystery of energy already.

As we open to new or increased sensory awareness we are offered experiences to correlate the inner instruction, or at least this is what I seemed to understand at the time. I remember walking down the hallway in the honor's dorm where I lived and being so sensitive that my body actually responded to the energy being emitted from others. It felt like I was pliable to a degree.

It was so dramatic in some cases that I found myself being pushed up against the opposite side of the hallway as I passed certain doors.

Others were less dramatic and those where no one was home presented no sensation at all or even a coldness of sorts. I could understand why some people choose to become reclusive or even hermits if they are unable to adjust their own sensory levels, like using an internal dial to turn down the sensitivity. Some people just go nuts.

If one was not aware or had no way of reflecting their experience to gain understanding, it surely would put them into a state of potential insanity. On the other hand I've heard that you have to be 'in' to be 'sane' when seeking spiritual enlightenment. Balance and harmony are key.

Perception Beyond the Doors

A couple of decades later when I had opened to this awareness again, I was taken off guard by a cute and quite open young woman, the daughter of my landlord at the time. I met her mother at a metaphysical organization business gathering. There was a disturbance, or argument, about the direction the organization should take. I was determined to assist in ways I knew worked.

I sat with a purple folder, information I brought to share, between my fingertips, breathing deeply and intending the equitable resolution of the issue. Ruthie, her mom, came up to me after the meeting and said, "I know you from long ago and I like what you are doing!" She recognized my 'peaceful' meditation, but I had no clue what she was talking about 'long ago.'

A few days later during a conversation with another friend that had attended the meeting, I mentioned I would soon need a place to live. She told me Ruthie had a guest house that had just been vacated and I should check into it. I moved in later that month.

Her daughter had moved back home after a divorce about a year later. Norma, our mutual friend, was delivering a microwave to Ruthie and needed help taking it inside. I happened to show up at the same time and she asked me if I could take it in for her. Gladly I did.

After I set the microwave down on Ruthie's kitchen counter, I turned to exit through the Arcadia door that opened to the back yard where the guest house was located. I had already been introduced to her daughter, but as I walked past her I was literally spun around by what felt like a hook in my solar plexus and below.

It was so noticeable that she offered an apology immediately. I didn't know what to say, so I just nodded my head and exited the house.

Back in college at Ball State another dramatic representation of these abilities and awareness came one weekend during the winter quarter, a couple of weeks before Christmas break. Gary and I were engaged in one of our trips together. We had realized that telepathy and telekinetic ability were present upon occasion, using our thoughts to reach out to each other no matter our location on campus.

There was a small group of others that we'd found that also were able to communicate beyond normal verbal ways, so I played with it by 'sending' a meeting place to the group and then checking to see if they would show up. There were always some who did. They would comment on the subtle impressions they got and just following them.

Perception Beyond the Doors

On several occasions they did arrive at the location, enough to affect belief in the process, meeting in places off the beaten path. But this night was a bit different. We had moved to the window of my room and were looking over toward the 8-story dormitory building across the street. We scanned the windows.

It was only a hundred yards or less away and we both noticed a couple of girls standing in their window. We could see their silhouettes in the window of the girls' dorm. I felt like they were in our heads, too. I hadn't said anything about it yet.

We had been conversing both verbally and in our 'telepathic' manner, but I kept hearing girls laughing. I had been hearing them and asked him verbally if he could hear them too. When I did, we both heard one of the voices say something like, "Silly boys, we've been listening to you for some time now. Didn't you know?"

And then the other spoke, "Why did you think we were laughing?" I couldn't believe it and told him so. Then I thought, "Well, if you've been listening, then let's make this for real and meet outside. Meet us in front of the dorm in five minutes." With that, Gary and I put our coats on and began our journey to the front door in great anticipation of meeting some cool chicks that could do this too.

When we reached the door and stepped outside they weren't there. I was bummed, but something attracted me to the side of the dorm between the dorm and cafeteria. I motioned to Gary and we walked toward the area. As soon as we turned the corner we noticed a dozen or so people lobbing snowballs back and forth without a word being spoken verbally.

As we approached the group, I recognized the voices of the girls and nearly instantly heard many more. We stayed and played for a while, but we never actually hooked up with the girls in person. I'm sure this was a pretty intimidating experience for all of us and most of us kept our distance.

It was bizarre enough just to fall into this experience, let alone try to articulate it verbally with any kind of rational thought. It was still pretty freakin' cool! There were rare moments where we could pass from telepathy to voice and back without breaking the stream of consciousness of our thoughts. It gave us the validation we needed.

I wondered if the Kingdom of Heaven was like this, so effortless in communication and transparent intent. Now, let me take this same consideration to another level of open communication.

What do you think about ghosts or spirits being able to show up through another's eyes? I mean using

Perception Beyond the Doors

another's body; one who is still alive. I don't expect you to believe it, but here's an interesting story nonetheless. Be prepared to have your mind bent.

Scott and I were discussing the boundaries or limits of telepathy. We had been experimenting with telepathy for some months, engaging a few others around campus. Scott and I were in a class called Futurisms and seemed to find each other instantly among the 200+ students in the lecture hall. It was kismet. He knew Gary as well.

It's funny how people enter your life when you open the door to a new experience. One of the things that intrigued me during college was not what was being taught, but what was going on with students who were hedging the edge of reality and stretching for experience, trying to understand a deeper life.

Hedging the edge includes investigating the senses deeper than waking consciousness. In order to do that, it is necessary to go beyond the waking consciousness into a deeper part of one's being. I found psychotropics to facilitate the process, much like many of those who sought to explore consciousness in years past but never found an ear with the public.

Regardless of the anti-drug propaganda over the decades, there seems to be some real merit in opening the doors to perception – just as Huxley found to be true in his day.

So one Saturday evening late in the spring Scott and I dropped just before dark and took a walk through the Christy Woods, the campus botanical gardens. It was only about a quarter-mile square, but it was enough to make a wonderful backdrop for a nice walk while we were waiting.

Christy Woods was about a 10-minute walk from the dorms. Scott's was just across the lane from mine. I think things started off when Scott asked me about the experience Gary and I had the last winter where Carolyn and I had shown up at his Grandfather's cabin in the middle of the night.

Gary had also told Scott about the telepathic event we'd experienced with the girls from the same dorm he and Scott lived in. He asked me if there were any limits to telepathy, specifically about distance and realm. I told him that I thought there were no boundaries, since there was no indication that focused thoughts would be dissipated over distances, no 'substance' has no resistance.

The only challenge would be the receiver, one who was tuned in to the thoughts of the sender or at least energetically open to them. This is a pseudo-science at best, so the discoveries usually aren't recorded,

Perception Beyond the Doors

let alone shared over any kind of a network until recently. Now information is being exchanged.

Back then there were no computer networks or the Internet to disburse our discoveries far and wide so the only kind available was neural nets at best, other minds that somehow were available to others. We had no idea about quantum realities or that what we had done was 'impossible' to many.

It was during that time that Dr. Hawking was exploring the nature of black holes, sometime before the introduction of M Theory, and even then it was all theory. Robert Monroe had just applied for patents for his Hemi-Sync® methods, so the idea of the benefits of altered states of consciousness was beginning to take hold at least.

Scott and I took up positions on opposite ends of my dorm room, lounging on the beds yet able to see each other easily. I don't recall what music we had on at the time, but as we gazed at each other in silence something happened quite unexpectedly. His body disappeared, with the exception of his eyes as this is where my focus of attention was at that moment. I just stared.

In semi-rapid succession several others appeared in his place, the eyes appearing to shift slightly in the process. I saw Jimi Hendrix, Lenny Bruce, Janice

Joplin, Jim Morrison and Marilyn Monroe just as plain as day, each remaining just long enough for me to recognize them.

I was able to observe without 'thinking' about what was happening. It was pretty freaky but at the same time quite comforting as there was no sense of trepidation. I just watched as each body transformed into the next in a kind of rhythm.

His body returned after Marilyn and his eyes immediate shifted to a widen look as though he was cognizant of something amazing happening. I asked him what had happened and he replied that he wasn't sure, but he knew he had left the room for a few moments. He could not describe where he had been. I told him what I'd seen during those moments and we both mused over the experience. Neither one of us could explain how or why.

Cosmic Conundrum Fulfilled

Institutions of higher learning provide such a plethora of potential for the personal perusal of possibilities in the paradigms of perspectives. In the second year of school I had changed my major from pre-med to psychology with a religion minor. I wanted to find out more about the connection between God and man, and the variety of ways that ones have journeyed inside in order to realize their own connections.

Quite often I found this to be the foundation of many religions. Someone had journeyed within themselves and found a way to express their connective tissue so that others might get a glimpse of the glory or profound peace it brings.

Well, that attempt has often also been turned into credos and memos of understanding between less scrupulous or wealthy individuals that desired domination of the population.

We have many of our organized religions to thank for that interesting display of human ego. Is there not a coherent message throughout?

School went okay for the first quarter, as I reacquainted myself with friends and the campus. My familiar partner in spiritual exploration was not present, though. I envied his vacation location. Gary was about 2,000 miles away in northern Canada with his grandfather, staying in a rustic old cabin with no modern conveniences.

I had called his parents a few times to inquire when he would be returning and each time it was, "Soon." They knew he would be back for winter quarter, just not the specific day. I was frustrated at not knowing when and my impatience paid off.

I returned from a date one Saturday morning, about 1 a.m. or so, and couldn't stop thinking about reaching out to Gary. I proceeded to test my telepathic ability a bit further. I had been thinking about the theoretical limits of telepathy, which were none that I knew of, and wondered if I could reach him. Why not?

I plugged in a tape by a band called 'White Witch' to a song called 'Help Me Lord.' It was quite spacey so I thought it would help set the tone. Again, music does many things to help us with our lives.

I lay down, closed my eyes, and began to picture his face in my mind's eye. It didn't take long before I was peering into his eyes, able to see his face as well. We gazed at each other for a moment, and then I imagined grabbing him by the shoulders and standing him up so that I could see his whole body. My visual perspective changed instantly as I could see his entire body now.

Cosmic Conundrum Fulfilled

It seemed to work as I felt a 'normal' connection and we discussed a few things about his return and a mutual girlfriend as well. She entered the conversational atmosphere as easily as we were talking with each other at the time. Her image was just as clear as his. We continued as a threesome for the duration of the song and as it completed, I felt it was time to disconnect as well.

So I said my goodbyes and I returned to the room and opened my eyes, going about he normal business of preparing for bedtime.

The following week was pretty normal and I decided to call his house on Friday evening to see if his parents had heard from him yet. To my amazement, he answered the phone and I could tell he was slightly out of breath.

I asked him where he'd been and what was happening. He had just pulled into the driveway when I called and knowing it was me on the phone, he ran in to answer it straightaway.

Cool… I told him I'd join him in a couple of hours. I was anxious to inquire.

Upon arrival, I talked with his parents for a short time regarding his trip and the advantages of being out in the wilderness for the summer. We got in my car to leave, a sporty orange Opel GT, and I asked him a rather open question to probe his mind. "Hey, did you catch any flack last weekend?" I said without any set-up as I wanted to leave the question open to anything.

He looked at me squarely in the eyes and said, "Yeah, you son of a bitch... you woke me up out of bed! I was lying there sound asleep and felt someone grab my shoulders and set me up in bed. As I opened my eyes your face was right in front of me, you f…r."

He went on, "Carolyn's face was right behind yours. We talked for a few and then you two split. I don't remember what we talked about, but I new you were there. It was pretty f..n' bizarre!"

I then told him what I'd done and we both just sat there wide-eyed and awed by the experience. About a week later, he got a postcard from Carolyn. It was one of those touristy postcards from a Krishna Camp in California.

All that was on the postcard was a circled address among many (a location in Santa Barbara, California) and at the bottom was written... "Enjoyed the conversation," in her hand writing. Nothing else was on the card at all. Neither one of us had heard from her since the end of spring quarter, some months previous.

Cosmic Conundrum Fulfilled

Imagine if something like that happened to you. What would you do?

Shortly thereafter, I bought a couple of drum sets and put them together as one in my dorm room. They were both Slingerland models, only a few years apart… about 25 or so…and all wood. I didn't care about the mis-match. I just wanted to play on a huge drum set.

The antique kit still had its original calf-skin heads, which I didn't have the sense to remove and keep. I broke most of them in just a few days. I stripped them down to bare wood so that at least they would look similar and replaced all the heads. Man, I was having fun!

The older set had a 24" bass so I took the newer 20" bass and made a floor tom out of it…a 9 piece kit in all, with 6 cymbals including a nice thick Zildjian 21" ride that had a wonderful ping ring. The kit was huge and I was ecstatic! I cut classes and practiced 6 to 8 hours a day using my album collection to learn to copy riffs and styles. It didn't take long to learn.

Neal Peart, Alan White, Aynsley Dunbar, John Bonham, Graham Edge, Lenny White, Danny Seraphine and more where quite helpful in my formative development. I'm sure it was brutal on my dorm mates while I was in the learning stages. I'd played before so I wasn't totally bereft of skill.

Surprisingly I picked it up pretty quick and reached a fair level of proficiency.

During that same time, my paternal grandmother was in the hospital just off campus. After a few years of her claiming to have throat cancer, she finally got it and passed on within a few months. I visited her a couple of times before her passing.

One morning shortly after my last visit two hometown friends, also students, showed up before school. We used to get together before school because we had the same classes a couple of days a week. It was a great way to start the day.

They still lived at home and commuted, so we would meet in my room and 'get ready' to go to class together. One of the guys was the nephew of David Star, the original owner of the older drum set. David had passed many years prior.

I was sitting on the floor in front of my base drum, leaning up against it. One of the guys was on a loveseat that we'd procured from the lobby and the other was sitting on my bed. As we were sitting and talking, among other things, I felt three finger pokes in between my shoulder blade just to the left of my spine. I noticed the time – 7:30 am.

Cosmic Conundrum Fulfilled

Without hesitation I told the two that Grandma had just left this world. They looked at me kind with the weird look you might expect and so I told them about the pokes. Later that morning Dad called with the news. I told him I knew already and that she had passed at about 7:30.

He asked me how I knew. I told him about the pokes. He was silent for a moment and I could feel his concern about my sanity. It was really hard for him to discuss this event or how I was able to know.

One evening some time later I was having difficulty picking up one of Neal's riffs on Rush's **Fly by Night** album. I went over and over and over it for some time. I just knew I could get it but it was an elusive pattern to say the least. I paused to think about how I might be able to 'tune in' to the pattern better. Then it occurred to me.

I got the idea that maybe; just maybe, David Star could help from the other side somehow. I got real still and quiet for a moment and said internally, "David, man if you love these drums as much as I do, could you give me a hand here?"

As if by magic, I immediately felt a warm tingling sensation start at the top of my head and go clear through my body down to my feet. "Far out!"

I went over to the turntable and started the tune over yet again. I hit every note perfectly. Wow, what a rush…. Pun intended.

Some people might not be so open with their past. Hey, I figure the universe has no secrets and if you wanted to investigate deep enough, the information is out there. I'm not particularly proud of my choices, but I'm alive and still an eduholic with a penchant for sharing.

Beside the facts, somewhere I might save someone great pain and suffering by sharing this. At any rate, I'd been contemplating a way to get back to the Light I had experienced the year before, even though I was not on any 'drugs' at that time it happened. I was curious and, based on the past, realized there was no 'death' to fear.

I was dating an English professor's daughter at the time and we had experienced a few trips together already. One night after we had ingested a large amount of LSD I wanted to play for her while waiting for the effects to launch. I put on Led Zeppelin II and cued it up to Moby Dick, John Bonham's solo, which he started by playing with his hands, so I started there.

I played through the solo, starting with my hands, and by the time the tune was over I had sticks in hand and was a bit sweaty from the workout. The

Cosmic Conundrum Fulfilled

next tune, Bring It On Home, began and I kept playing along with the album. I was feeling pretty strange, though.

After a few moments I looked over at Betsy and as our eyes met something miraculous happened. Everything beyond the perimeter of the cymbals and drums went 'white.' I continued playing.

I could still see the drums, my body, and the floor beneath me as I continued to play. Somehow I knew it was okay because I could feel no physical disturbance and could think as I continued playing, although I wasn't thinking much as I played. It felt like I was completely free.

So I just continued along with the album. Within a few moments, my sight returned to normal and the rest of the room came back into view as I played through the end of the tune.

Betsy had a really weird look on her face that looked like a cross between complete awe and intense fear. I asked her what was up and she asked me where I had gone. Evidently I had disappeared for a few moments into this white light after our eyes had met and it really freaked her out. I could understand why.

I told her I had no idea where I had gone, but that I could still see the drums, cymbals, my body and the floor from my perspective, although I was surrounded by the white light, too. I'm not sure what it proved, if anything. All I know is that I had the same feeling of being 'home' in the light.

I had returned somehow, however surreptitiously, but I was there. It was a place of freedom, no fears of any kind, totally blissful and serene. I would not recommend this procedure to anyone. I was lucky, I suppose, to have a strong constitution.

Now there could be a number of valid explanations for what happened. I'm sure the clinicians would have a field day with it. The 'Spirit Molecule' folks would no doubt have a different story to tell, perhaps somehow creating a chemical bridge between this world and the next. Perhaps it was just some wild imaginings, but it was odd that the glance is what triggered the return to the 'light.'

Inappropriate Choices?

Of course I didn't tell my parents that I had used half of my room and board money for school to pay for drums. I didn't even tell them I had them. I didn't think about what I would do about my room and board situation when Christmas break came. I knew had to move out.

I had a car, so I could find a house off campus. But where and how? This meant that I had to move out of the dorm over winter break without their knowledge, too. I wasn't sure how I was going to do it. I thought maybe the paper would have an answer.

I scoured the Muncie Star and found a house with free rent. It was south of Muncie that I could live in for free. "Free?" you might ask. Well, it had no heat as no fuel oil had been purchased for the furnace and no running water because the pipes had already frozen a month before according to the owner on the phone. I didn't care. It was someplace to go.

There was electricity and another couple was living there already, so it was inhabitable. I guess the owner just wanted someone in the house. So I took the opportunity and made some plans. I figured it would work out somehow.

I knew that I could borrow some quilts and baseboard heaters from my maternal grandmother, who was still alive, to prepare one of the rooms. There was another couple living there already, oddly enough. They stayed for another week after I showed up and then moved on to warmer quarters I suspect. We didn't get that much of a chance to talk.

Even though I had a car, a '65 Skylark, I had help with moving from a couple friends. We took all my stuff; drums, stereo, albums, clothes, etc., and brought them to the house. I brought the quilts and three baseboard heaters from my grandmother's house. It wasn't much, but it would do for the time.

Needless to say I needed a support network to make it through this transition. I had no idea how it was going to happen. It was quite an interesting production indeed. On a good day you could barely see your breath in the living room.

I was still going to school, having sold some albums to get enough money to fill my gas tank, driving back and forth to school on a daily basis. Gas was around $.50 a gallon so I didn't need much. Sometimes others would join me, but I was usually by myself. It was a really deplorable situation and I knew I needed to do something about it. But, what?

As much as I was in denial about my situation, I still hung out on campus and with friends after school. One Friday evening I joined some friends at an Apple Scruffs meeting (Beatles fan club) to watch

Inappropriate Choices?

the monthly movies shown in one of the lecture halls on campus. I was glad to be in a warm environment and among some friends.

The 250-seat auditorium was about two-thirds full. Magical Mystery Tour was first up and Yellow Submarine was next. About half-way through Yellow Submarine an idea hit me like a freight train and surprisingly, I felt like a weight was taken off my shoulders as a result.

I was not particularly thinking about how to change my situation at that moment, but the idea came anyway. I really did need some help.

The thought was to go down to the front of the room after the movie was over and introduce myself as Billy Shears. At first I thought it was nuts. I certainly was not Billy, nor did I think it was a particularly sane move on my part.

Beatle's fans know who Billy was... to the rest of you - he was the leader of Sergeant Pepper's Lonely Hearts Club Band.

After contemplating it a bit and arguing with myself I thought it might be a great way to get an immediate support group that could help me with food, laundry and a much needed shower, even though I knew I was only 'acting as if' I was him.

I really had nothing to lose, so I walked down to the front of the room, turned to face the audience that was just beginning to leave and announced, "Hi, I'm Billy Shears." I noticed there were several guys still sitting in the front row that started crying, like tears of joy. It was pretty cool, but weird.

That was a bit bewildering, but I suppose somehow they might have been thinking about Billy Shears actually showing up. Maybe that was what prompted the thought in the first place. I certainly believe I wouldn't have come up with the idea on my own. Thoughtmospheric conditions?

After a few moments of milling about, I walked outside with my friends, who were understandably a bit shocked at what I'd done. They didn't have much time before a group of people assembled around me. I didn't need to embellish on the Billy Shears thing but wondered how to tell them I needed some help.

I found that I didn't even have to voice my needs as I got all kinds of offers to come visit, hang out, and party or whatever. I found everything I needed and more, at least for a short time. It worked to perfection. I wondered what would happen if I told them the truth.

Christmas break was the following week so I spent a few days at home with my parents, unable to tell them of my stupidity and thinking nothing about the severity of my living conditions at the house.

I'm sure they knew something was amiss, but I was in my defiant days and wouldn't talk to them much at the time. I wanted to get away from them as soon as I could. So I did. Looking back as a parent and grandfather now I'm sure it was excruciating for them, knowing they could not reach me in that state of mind. Still, it was my life at the time.

I was able to get back and forth to the house in my '65 Skylark (I even got some gas money) and still attend classes. The winter quarter had started up again after Christmas break.

The first week of January I was on my way back into school with some friends after going out to the house to get some books. We turned a corner and were soon confronted by a black Rambler headed straight for us. It had snowed the night before and the streets were icy still. I swerved to miss it only to hit something else.

I missed the Rambler only to clip off an old telephone pole that had been replaced, having it fall right in the center of the top of the car. The new pole was just far enough away that I didn't hit it. The old pole had put a nice crease not only in the front of the car, but in the roof after it came crashing down on it.

Of course the car was totaled even though we'd only been traveling about 20 miles per hour when we hit the pole. Fortunately no one was hurt. It all happened in slow motion and we joked about it as we stood waiting for the police to show up.

I was really bummed that the only transportation I had was now gone. I couldn't waste time in my misery, though. I quickly made some phone calls and had a ride from some of Betsy's friends, at least for a while.

We were all fine and after the tow truck took the car away we walked the rest of the way to school, only about a mile. It was at least sunny out, although in the high 30s, so the walk was semi-enjoyable. I spent that night at a friend's house, went to school the next day and then got a ride back out to the house. I wasn't sure how to proceed.

I got rides for the rest of the week, but I wondered how I would continue getting to school the next week. That weekend the weather got worse. It was getting really cold, snowing and the wind was howling through the poorly sealed windows that Sunday night. I didn't even think about *not* going to school the next day.

Monday morning I awoke at about 5 a.m. to the radio alarm only to hear the radio DJ talking about the 77 below zero wind-chill factor. He was commenting on the severity of the cold – breaking a 100-year record. We were also getting some snow still, but even with minimal amounts it was creating 'white-out' conditions for driving. I still had to make it to school.

I could see my breath even with the heaters on. I grabbed my clothes and put them under the blankets with me to warm them up. I knew that I would have to get to school somehow, so I got dressed with several layers of clothing. I walked through a couple of feet of snow and really hard wind up to the highway that was about a half a mile away, hoping to hitch a ride.

To my delight and surprise, I got a ride rather quickly from a couple that was returning from an Edgar Winter concert in Indianapolis. They dropped me off at the intersection of the highway going into town at around 5:30. The wind was mind numbing and as I stood alongside the road with my thumb out, I started to feel my fingers and toes tingle; the first signs of frostbite.

I started walking with my thumb out, holding my collar tightly around my neck as I walked directly into the wind's force. My arms and legs were beginning to feel the effects of the cold and the wind felt like it was blowing right through my clothing. I noticed my fingers and toes were beginning to feel numb and I began to get concerned for my life.

Now at those temperatures and in that condition I had to make some quick decisions, although it seemed excruciatingly long. I suddenly felt the terror of a life-threatening situation. I figured I had a couple of choices - keep walking and possibly freeze to death or stand out in the road to get a car to stop. I wasn't going to last.

Obviously they could not see me alongside the road as several cars had passed by without stopping. Looking back I'm sure they couldn't even see in front of them very far, let alone notice someone on the side of the road in the dark with their headlights being refracted through the blinding snow.

I was taking a chance at getting hit, but I had to do something, I knew I would die from exposure if I didn't. The traffic wasn't moving but a few miles an hour, so I figured I had a good chance of surviving even if I did get hit.

I hated my choices, my position, and my life at that moment. I was so angry with myself and my condition that I didn't care about stepping out into traffic and was ready to give it up. I just wanted out of the cold.

So I stepped out in front of the next car and prayed they would stop. They did, fortunately. A Ford station wagon stopped and the passenger door opened. I ran around to the side and jumped in, immediately voicing my thankfulness for his consideration. I was safe for the moment.

My first obstacle, the fierce storm, was now outside and I was warm again. I felt safe temporarily and I was totally thankful for the result of my steps.

My savior was an older guy on his way to pick up newspapers from the newspaper office and deliver them to customers. He looked a bit concerned although he did not pry. He asked where I was headed and I told him I needed to get to school. It was still really early and he asked me why I was trying to get there in this ridiculous weather. I wasn't sure how to answer.

I told him I wanted to give myself plenty of time to make it there because I wasn't sure how long it would take in these conditions. I told him about an IHOP close to campus that I could get a cup of tea (I didn't drink coffee yet) before heading to my first class at 7:30 am.

He gave me a ride all the way there, even though it was out of his way. I had enough change for a cup of tea, so I warmed up and knew I would catch my first class on time. It was about 6:00.

After warming up a bit I walked over to my old dorm and sat down at the piano in the lounge. For about a half an hour I plunked at the keys, imagining I was creating some mystical piece reflecting the situation I was going through. It wasn't much at all, just a few chords and single keys struck in randomness, like some of the new age music I heard decades later.

I had no idea how to play the notes, but the song in my head was bittersweet. It let me pass the time in quiet desperation. I went on to class wondering how the hell I was going to make it through the day. I had something to do and someplace to be so it was good enough to start me on my way.

It wasn't surprising that only a few other students, probably as insane as me, were in class that morning or anytime that day for that matter. I attended the Philosophy 200 class first at 7:30, then the Psych 301 (Statistics) around 11 and finally my Comparative Religions class at 1:30. The campus bookstore and student commons were close so I spent my off hours there. Fortunately I met up with some friends that bought me some food and drink. Later in the day I went over to a girl's dorm to visit a girl I'd befriended at the Beatles movies. We hung out talking until midnight curfew and I had to leave.

Inappropriate Choices?

I walked across the street to a frat house. I hated frat rats and never considered going to one of their houses on campus. What the hell was I thinking? Well, it was about the only place where I might find some shelter at that time of night. It was still intensely cold and I needed shelter. Billy Shears had lost his network.

I'd never been in a frat house before. I walked up and knocked on the door. I was dumbfounded and so grateful when a classmate opened the door. I never figured him for a frat rat because his hair was almost as long as mine. At that time my hair was down past my shoulders and my beard was a few inches long as well. Hippies and frat rats didn't get along at all in those days.

We had *Statistics 101* together, so I had seen him earlier in the day. We had gotten to know each somewhat in class and had spent some time throwing the Frisbee at the beginning of winter quarter during some nicer weather. He wasn't quite the jock by appearance, so I was a bit shocked, although thankful, when he answered the door. I still can't help but think it was a divine intervention in disguise. It was totally random for me, though.

Nevertheless he invited me in and asked if I'd like to go downstairs and play some pool. On the way he asked what the hell I was doing out on a night like this and I was honest - looking for some place to crash for the night. I was out of options and this was the closest place to look for relief from the weather. I had no idea what I was going to find.

The house was three stories with a huge basement, part of 'frat row' which was along the main east-west street through the center of campus. I followed him through the house and down the stairs to the basement where there was a recreation room.

I was again pleasantly surprised when I saw an old girlfriend standing in front a jukebox with another guy. It looked like she was having a rather heated discussion with him, but I said 'hi' (and she responded) on the way toward the pool table.

Once there I started racking the balls while my host got a cue. After I finished and on the way to get my cue, he asked me if I'd like some electric Kool-Aid. My eyebrows went up and I nodded an affirmation. He walked over to the refrigerator and pulled out a gallon jug about half-full of red Kool-Aid.

We played a few of games of 8-ball and finished the jug in the process.

I had to relieve myself by that time so I asked where the restroom was, got directions and headed upstairs to find it. I was feeling good that I'd found a place to hang out, at least for the time being.

Inappropriate Choices?

I was inside and warm.

While on my way to the restroom I heard someone yelling obscenities and threats, but I wasn't sure at whom. I looked up to see a guy about twice my size practically running across the balcony floor and down the stairs toward me. He was yelling at me. I remember something like, "What the hell are you doing here m...f...r? I'm gonna kick your ass!"

By the time he was done with the last sentence he was at the base of the stairs and in front of me. Evidently he didn't like my being there and while continuing to verbally assault me he literally picked me up by the back of my shirt and belt, carried me over to a door with a metal bar across it, kicked it open and threw me up the stairs leading to the ground level.

I pleaded with him to at least let me get my coat and hat. I knew better than to challenge him. He refused to allow me to get my things and hoisted me up the stairwell with a "Get the f.. out of here and stay out. If I see you again I'll kill you, you f..n loser. I mean it!" What would you have done?

It is not power that corrupts, but fear.
Aung San Suukyi

Undisturbed calmness of mind is attained by cultivating friendliness toward the happy, compassion for the unhappy, delight in the virtuous, and indifference toward the wicked.

Patnjali

Taking My Chances

Well, I desperately needed my coat and hat (it was still sub-zero), so I tried to sneak in the front door to find them. They were down in the basement close to the pool table, perhaps. I really didn't know. I made it to the top of the basement stairs.

He saw me again and repeated his previous motions, this time following me up the stairs. His eyes were angry and violent and I wasn't sure what was going to happen as he came toward me.

I had no idea how to get out of this one so I took an open stance and told him all I wanted was my coat and hat and I'd be gone in a heartbeat. He snarled and swore at me as he continued toward me again, looking very menacing.

As if it would help, I asked, "Don't you know who I am?" I thought it might at least get him to stop and think. I wasn't the slightest bit concerned about being Billy Shears or even that he'd heard of the name. I just wanted him to stop and think.

That comment seemed to fuel the fire and he moved faster toward me, backing me up against a small sports car in the parking lot a few yards away from the top of the stairs. There was no way I could fight him. The size difference was ridiculous.

He took a swing at me and connected with my left eye. I tried to get out of the way, only to find myself launching backwards onto the hood of the car, sliding off and into the snow. I picked myself up and backed away from him, tripping over an unseen curb, falling backward into the snow. He pounced on me immediately and as he drew his arm back to strike me again, someone grabbed it and pulled him off of me. I looked up to see it was a campus policeman. Whew!

What happened next was a little weird. There were several cops and they started asking others what had happened. One of them asked me for my identification and I handed him my school ID and he began writing on an index card that was on a clipboard. I asked the one that had helped me up if I could go get my coat and hat because I was freezing. It was still way below zero.

He walked me to the front door where two other guys and my friend were standing. My friend said he'd go get my coat and hat. While I was there waiting, the two others grabbed me by the arms, extended them out, and lifted me off the floor a bit while pinning me against the wall.

They weren't being violent, but they definitely wanted to show me they were not letting me go. My eyebrow was cut pretty bad, dripping blood down the front of my face and onto my sweater. It had a really weird vibe if you know what I mean, feeling like I was about ready to get crucified or something, especially with the blood trickling down the front of my face.

My friend came back with my coat and hat and the two put me down and followed me outside. My eye obviously needed stitches so the campus cops took me to the hospital from there. They were curious about why I was there to say the least. They seemed a bit pensive, too.

I didn't think it telling a long story was appropriate so I told them I was just looking for a place to stay warm for the night. The hospital was only a couple of blocks away so it didn't take us long to get there. I was taken in to the emergency room, ushered to a bed where they cleaned me up and stitched up my eye and sent me to the waiting area.

I found the Dean of Admissions (a personal friend of Dad's) sitting in the room waiting for me. I tried to talk with him a bit even though I could tell he was more than just a little upset. I could see the concern in his eyes as well.

Heck, it was 3 am by this time. I'd be angry too. He told me that Dad was on his way and he'd be there soon. Dad showed up about a half hour later. We sat in relative silence until then. My head was reeling from what I'd been through the last few days and I wasn't sure what was going to happen.

By the time he arrived, I was so relieved to see Dad that I didn't think a thing about what I'd just gone through, only that he was there and I felt safe now. Rather than being able to leave, he advised me that I needed to stay there for a bit. I thought with a blow to the head and possible concussion, overnight observation might be in order so I did not resist.

I found out later Dad had told him that I was on the edge and needed a watchful eye. In turn the Dean had told the campus police that if my name ever came up he was to be called immediately. So there he was at 3 am after getting a call. He was a good friend to Dad. We all need friends like that.

What soon became apparent, though, was that it was not just overnight observation. A couple of orderlies escorted me onto an elevator and up to the seventh floor, where there was a very large black man 'guarding' a door. I knew I was in trouble then. I would be there for some time.

The guard stood up from the chair next to the door, grabbed a wad of keys from his belt and said, "Ah, got another one for me, huh?" He put a key in the door and opened it. The orderlies took me inside down a hallway and into an empty room on the right. They weren't gentle but they weren't treating me like a convict either.

Shortly thereafter, my shoes, belt, necklace and pants were removed. I argued with them as they were stripping my pants off, but to no avail. I was given two shots (one in each butt cheek) and the next thing I knew I woke up hours, possibly days, later with a very full bladder and need of relief.

I had to pee so badly, but both the door to the bathroom and the hallway were locked. I banged on the room door for what seemed like hours and nobody came. I eventually urinated in the corner because I couldn't hold it any longer. I was so embarrassed, but I really had no choice. There wasn't even a waste basket in the room.

I had no idea what time or day it was at that point as it was dark out. Several hours later a nurse came in to check on me and brought me some food. Another few hours went by and I finally spoke to a doctor. By this time it was light out.

I told him what had happened as briefly as possible, but be probed more for the long version and I reluctantly provided it, including the part about Billy Shears. I knew I wasn't crazy, so I was completely open with him, thinking he'd be like Dr. Abell, or at least similar.

The nurse brought me in a pink liquid a little later and told me the doctor wanted me to drink it. I was not allowed out of the room. I couldn't understand why, but they kept telling me everything would be fine. I found out later that I was being assessed and their procedure was to keep me isolated until the determination of my treatment. The pink liquid was Thorazine, a powerful anti-psychotic drug.

I was moved to a room, a few days later, shared with two other guys. Once I got out of solitary confinement there were others on the floor that seemed to really have some mental problems. I soon realized that I was getting a glimpse of reality few experience. I wasn't sure how long I would be there, but it sure was an eye opener into a population often hidden from view.

There was this really short guy that would squat in the middle of the hall while yelling out, "Two dogs!" Another woman paced back and forth talking to herself in several tones of voice. There was another guy that reminded me of Prince Valiant because of the way his hair was cut. He was quite soft spoken and kind.

I think I was the youngest one on the ward and others seemed to try to look out for me. I had no idea how long I would be there or what the pink liquid was I was taking four times a day.

Taking My Chances

I soon learned I had been prescribed 2,000mg of Thorazine (500mg 4 times a day in a liquid suspension) because I had been diagnosed as a manic depressive paranoid schizophrenic. Could they find more? Jeez....

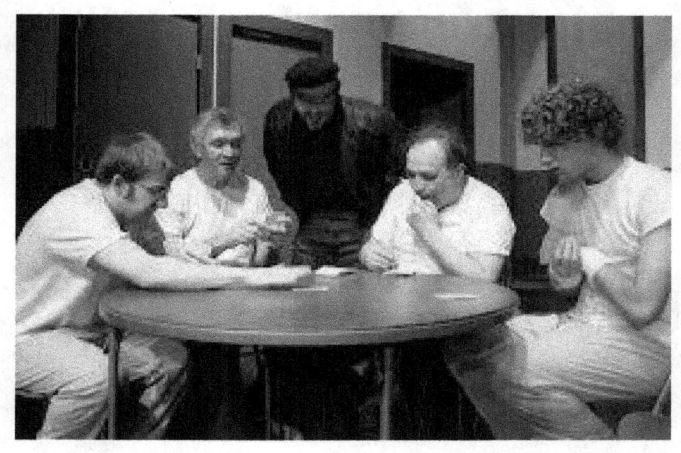

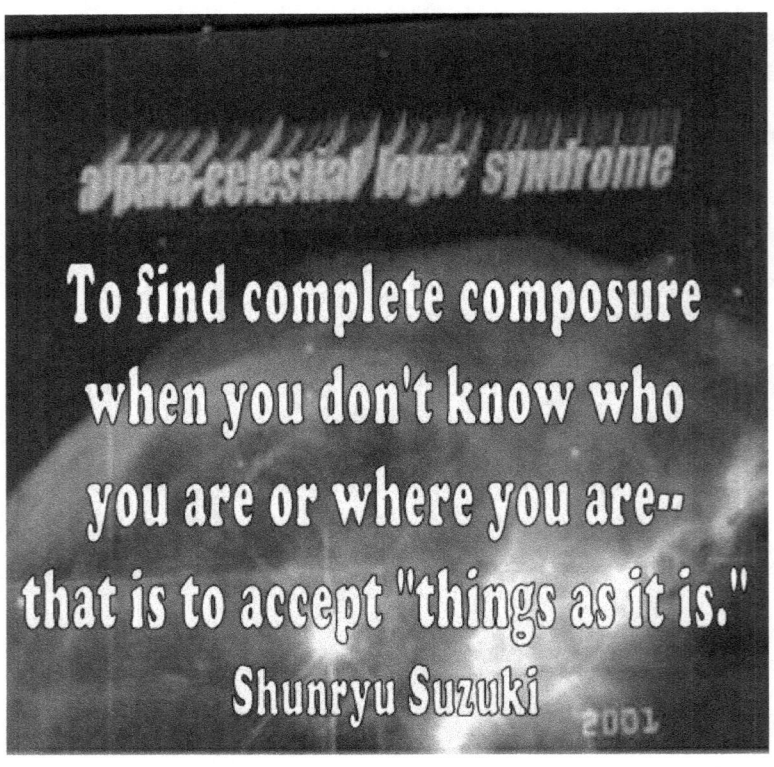

Let us look at a humble virtue, that of gratitude. With this virtue alone, the world could be at peace.

Buddhadasa Bhikkhu

A Separate Reality

As much as I attempted to explain the logic of my actions the doctor wasn't buyin' it, no matter how I tried to explain it. I also told him about the 'white light' experience from the year before. That went over like a led zeppelin.

It became painfully obvious that 'my' truth did not matter and that his 'expertise' held the most weight. I grew to appreciate his point of view, although it wasn't pleasant.

I was taken to court for a competency hearing after about a week in the hospital where I spilled my guts, knowing I wasn't crazy and this was all just a big mistake. I thought I explained myself fairly well and this would all be over soon. It worked just the opposite. Now I really understood what Dr. Abell had meant.

I spent days in the music room, mostly, listening to albums and sometimes talking with the other 'inmates.' Most of the people were really nice, but some of them were hard to understand when they engaged their 'psychosis' or whatever put them there. I never felt in danger with anyone, though.

The nice thing was there were no fights, except with some of the nurses trying to subdue patients that were a little out of control. That was hard to watch.

Seeing someone being restrained that I knew just wanted to be loved was hard to take.

I'd play ping pong for an hour or so just about every day as 'exercise' and make fun of the male nurses that thought they could beat me. Sometimes they could, but I usually held my own. We had a ping pong table in the garage for several years and I loved to play.

I found out I wasn't supposed to be able to do that according to the 'treatment' scenario if I was truly responding to it under the diagnosis deemed relevant. My quickness wasn't completely there or I would've been demolishing them. They certainly weren't trying to let me win. These male nurses were very competitive when playing.

I could definitely hold my own even on medication. I should have been a lump in the corner being on that much Thorazine. I didn't know any better though, and just went on like I was being as normal as possible. I didn't know what to expect.

Years later while teaching exceptional (special ed) students I understood the diagnose/treat/monitor scenario much deeper, but with little change in attitude toward its usefulness. I taught special education in high school for a couple of years.

I learned that the only way the doctors could tell if the medication they prescribed was doing what it was supposed to do was by observing the teenager's behavior. There were and are no blood tests to determine the right cocktail. It's hit or miss when it comes to most treatment plans.

One night in the hospital I got a phone call. The nurse said they weren't allowed to let patients use the floor phone. It was the only one I ever got there. I didn't get to answer it but the nurse told me her name. There was a girl with a similar name that I dated a couple of times after breaking up with my high school sweetheart.

I never thought much about her phone call, although I did think it was a nice gesture to try to reach out to me. I had prayed for a soul mate, too, and it happened to be the night before the girl had called. I was curious of the timing, but still held some reservations. I remained open to the possibility and also knew that I wasn't ready for any relationship yet. I wasn't ready for much of anything.

One thing did happen that was most notable for the record. Mom only came to visit me once during my entire stay at the Ball Memorial hotel. Dad told me later that she was too emotional over my institutionalization that she couldn't bring herself to come see her 'sick' son. Well, one night she did show up unannounced.

About a half an hour before she got there, my tongue swelled up and my right foot became curled in like I had a club foot. It wasn't a muscle cramp because it didn't hurt. My tongue was so swollen that I could barely speak and my words came out so thick they practically drooled off my lips, but even without the drool they were nearly inaudible. I was so embarrassed.

So Mom shows up a little later and I'm in that condition still. I was so embarrassed because I had absolutely no physical side-effects whatsoever, except weight gain, before this night and the new side-effects had started just before she came to visit, about the time she would have started her journey from home.

I was not thinking that deeply at all at the time, only that I was sorry she had to see me in that condition. I could tell by the look in her eyes that she was just devastated by seeing me like that. As a parent and grandparent now, I can empathize even more with the feeling of despair.

She sat with me a while and told me some news about family things, so I didn't have to try to talk a lot. I hurt so bad inside then. She soon needed to leave so I escorted her down the hall to the door as best I could. I went to bed shortly afterward and woke up the next morning with no more side-effects; my tongue was fine and my foot was normal again. "Weird," I thought, but didn't take it any further for the moment.

Now I had been sensitive to feelings as a child, but picking up on Mom's energy and manifesting a 'sick' son for her to witness was a new trick. There was no medical reason for my side effects.

It happened during a very traumatic emotional period, my mother having to face her fear in the moment, and a wide-open empath could very easily manifest that strong of a projection, especially with the emotional cording already in place. I had to consider the obvious.

A week or so later I was up late one night, sitting at the table in the common area when a large vivacious Black woman came up and asked if she could join me at the table. I welcomed her and she sat down to my left and opened a rather nondescript looking book, bound in brown leather. It looked old, sacred and well used.

I was reading a Bible at the time as well. There wasn't much other material to read that was of interest. I found some solace in reading from it by spontaneously opening the book and just letting my eyes drift to a passage. I'd start there and read for a bit. It was always uplifting.

After reading for a few minutes we began talking, sharing our reasons for being there. She had been talking to others about being a 'white witch' and soon found herself being submitted to psychological evaluation. I inquired about what a 'white witch' was; reminded of the album I used to contact Gary earlier that school year.

She told me about Wiccan beliefs in general and I'll synopsize them here:

1. *Live in harmony with nature, the world, and people.*
2. *Respect all paths whether or not you agree with them. Do not impose your own beliefs upon others through acts of evangelism or conversion.*
3. *Respect your body, and keep it healthy and pure through practices such as exercise, healthy eating, and meditation.*
4. *Celebrate life and living. Don't just exist.*
5. *Attune with the cycles of the earth.*
6. *Respect all people, regardless of sex, age, race, culture, class and religion.*
7. *Respect and revere the God and Goddess in their many forms.*
8. *Always focus on learning and understanding for personal growth through reading, practicing your craft, and accepting the advice and wisdom of others.*

9. Harness and develop your power and nurture a kind of union with the gods and powers of nature.

10. Create balance in your own life by embracing all the above.

Now I remember being fascinated by the Wiccan beliefs. It was not one of the religions I had read about in my earlier quests, but it seemed to embody them all in a much cleaner philosophy.

I told her what had happened to me, starting with the white light and including being taken to court for a competency hearing. She took a very deep breath, paused in thought for a few moments and then asked if she could give me a blessing. Absolutely! I was up for any assistance in my predicament.

Bring it on!

She excused herself for a minute, got up and went to her room. She returned with a small vial of oil, said a short prayer, moistened her fingertip with the oil and made a cross on my forehead, leaving a trace of the oil. I felt blessed.

I had a similar blessing from the Rev. Dr. Charles Brown (spiritual guide for Understanding Principles for Better Living Church – founded by Della Reese) a couple of decades later.

I truly felt 'blessed' by her genuine intention for my well-being and her acceptance of my 'story.' The next morning was my weekly appointment with the hospital psychiatrist. I had continued a similar theme throughout, hoping someday he would actually listen.

The next day I shifted from the old storyline. I began telling Dr. Yarling what he wanted to hear, evidently. I admitted to everything he suspected, somehow, and must've been very convincing regarding my shift in mindset. He seemed more pleased than usual.

A few days later I was told they were going to begin reducing my dosage and I would be out in three weeks. My favorite nurse, Betty (a cute petite black woman), told me Yarling had said something about a 'miracle' cure... I'd come out of my psychosis.

Did I have any 'success' in my treatment? I really didn't feel any different about my personal experiences, other than pretty stupid for not talking to my parents about the drums and my financial condition. It might have saved me losing my album and 8-track tape collection, not to mention the quadraphonic stereo.

I felt like I'd just lied to the psychiatrist in order for him to deem me 'sane,' even though it solved the problem. My real questions were still about my experiences I knew I was just one person, Bruce, and Billy Shears was a totally fabricated ploy for attention… worked.

All of a sudden, after prostrating myself in total submission, I had a 'miracle' cure (he'd told my parents he wasn't sure I would ever come out of 'it') and I was released a few weeks later, still on some massive doses of Thorazine and 50 pounds heavier. I felt and looked swollen, my body image was gross at that point.

I was a bit emaciated when I went in (125 lbs.), but the 175 pounds I carried when I left was 35 pounds over my normal weight and it looked like all water. I didn't even look like me I was so puffy. It came off in time thank God. Now I'm back up to that weight, but I look like it fits as I've gotten older. I'd like to lose some.

The result of all of this was my self-esteem was temporarily absent, no confidence at all and it would be some time before I felt 'comfortable' as *me* again. I got severely anxious for quite a while. When I spoke to people I would shake on the inside so bad that sometimes my body would physically tremble. It was quite embarrassing.

It took me some time to recognize that I could control the fear of rejection, even though I just wanted to be accepted and heard as being authentic and real. I thought 'quivering' was in fear of rejection or misunderstanding I guess.

I learned later that it might not have been my own feelings I was responding to – others had similar sensations when being confronted with experiences beyond their direct knowing.

I suppose it could have been because of the withdrawal from the Thorazine, too. Over time, through years of focused work and serendipitous opportunity, I gradually rose back into the person I knew before the brief hospital visit, or at least someone recognizable as a shadow of my former self. I liked that person a lot and so did everyone else. I hoped I could ascend from my first set of trials and tribulations.

I had been involved in many high school activities, some in front of several thousand people, so I was no stranger to exposure. One of the neatest was doing a solo trampoline performance as part of a circus act for a half-time show during one of our basketball games.

I was a real ham at heart, I suppose. When I was a lifeguard I performed some pretty spectacular dives during the breaks, too. I loved having the audience and sometimes people would even clap.

My favorite was a reverse 2 ½ with a half-twist. An uncle told me some years later that he tried to get a diving coach from IU to come to Alexandria to watch me dive. He thought I deserved a good look, but it never happened.

In everything I attempted that was challenging I was a bit nervous at times, but I never felt like I was shaking on the inside so strongly that I just knew it was visible on the outside.

It was tremendously disheartening to go through that depth of insecurity. I was determined to rise again, just like the Phoenix, and fulfill my destiny as was told to me so short a time ago.

I was engaged in some reckless behavior, no doubt. Looking back I was amazed at how 'protected' I was in those days. Now it is important to note that I was fully aware that this was an act and I did not have any false notions that I was Billy Shears. It was a purposeful deception of a group for my own personal needs.

The only reason it did not continue was because I got lucky at the frat house and was 'committed' by my parents in an act of desperation for protecting or saving my life. It took me years to forgive them, but after my own children I have such great respect for their ability and decisions to act when they did. I'd gone too far. They stepped in when I could not.

I also considered that, because I'd focused more on the personal or self-aggrandizement during my second year at school that the events were a warning. I had stepped outside the realms of service to others and my intent to be honest and sincere in 'The Work' brought consequences beyond my understanding at the time.

The Messy Antic Complex

The uniqueness of my entrance into the White Light and the ensuing experience made me vulnerable to an ego-centered, although well-intended, bantering that many with similar experiences have fallen prey to over the centuries. *A personal experience is interpreted as being important for sharing with the world...the message is what is important.*

As with many others, the first human place in consciousness was to want to announce to the world that I AM HERE, believing that I AM THE ONE. After all, I was told I was to work with these 'points of light' to facilitate a new world order. If it is true, then I need to tell others about it, right? ...NOT! At least not before distilling it for the public.

That was the beginning of what the field of psychology calls the 'messiah complex.' This is where one sets themselves up as a self-proclaimed messiah. I was not intentionally setting out to do so, yet I have to admit that it would sound like it to many. No matter how little the ego is, people often don't hear it from the same place it is spoken.

I would imagine that if I was listening to me, I'd have to agree it sounded a bit self-prognosticative. That would seem to be the historical pattern as well.

What do we do?

However, like Howard Bloom's scientific exploration of history, religious leaders tend to manipulate masses of people in order to crush any resistance to their 'truth.' I'm glad I let go of the desire to even be considered as a spiritual leader, if only because I didn't feel educated enough or experienced enough to be an effective leader.

Since that time, I've observed a paradox that claiming identity is only a consequence of having a huge ego, and yet to some it is a **major** consequence. As one of the many paradoxes in the discovery of Self, I'll elaborate further and hopefully shed some light on the subject (pun intended). It is probably one of the most profound realizations one can have on the path of discovery. It is the discovery of Self.

As seekers of truth progress in consciousness we see the goal as Cosmic Consciousness (many other terms could be used) or so we believe. What is that exactly? *Cosmic consciousness* is the concept that the universe is a living superorganism with which animals, including humans, interconnect and form a collective consciousness which spans the cosmos.[2]

In order to truly find it, one has to let go of everything held within the sphere of attachments -

---

[2] http://en.wikipedia.org/wiki/Cosmic_consciousness

The Messy Antic Complex

beliefs included. Experience, both internal and external, is the ultimate teacher in establishing a congruent reality that balances our inner and outer polarities, bringing a state of harmony – within and without. We can share that if/when we choose.

Now it would be easy to see how one with such a profound experience at such a young age would attach himself to this belief, not realizing its fullness. There are many, both male and female, who have reached a state of consciousness where they believe themselves to be THE ONE.

People who've been affected also become so attached to this identity that their focus becomes telling everyone else that they are THE ONE, whether verbally or nonverbally, and espousing grandiose concepts of living in love without providing so much as a shred of evidence of their ability to do so. Living in love is important indeed.

The thing is, it's all a repeat of what happened several times throughout history and yet we attach ourselves to an incongruent and inconsistent belief that God works through one person. We are all connected. We all have a direct connect to God.

We also must realize that this identity thing is great, but we make it too great. We are all Cosmic, we are all Christ, or as I have learned from the Mayan "In lak' esh... I am another you." The Hindus use 'Namaste' as "the Divine in me recognizes the Divine in you."

In spite of that awareness, "Yeah, but I AM THE ONE!" resounds internally in many still, leading others down the path to destruction such as is happening with the current world leaders believing they are acting according to God's Will when it is quite obvious that the nature of love, to care for one another, is not in the picture according to the basic premises of love.

Okay, so you are THE ONE. What's next?

What do you do?

How do you act?

Moreover, how do you LEAD?

Once you realize that you are Christ, or even God or Goddess to some, then what is next?

You are still here, still in a body, still within the world of physicality and its natural laws and order. We are unaware of the greater still.

What's the catch?

Well, the catch is that ONE turn into MANY, rising above their own identity issues to collaborate with others to actually do something about manifesting this new living awareness we call LOVE. At this phase, identity becomes a non-issue. Jobarchy rules... the job is the boss and everybody wins. Ego becomes Wego.

We all know of our paths and THE WORK. Well, maybe not but work with me here. Why do you think it is called that...The Work? Wouldn't it make sense that all this talk about the 'Cultural Creatives' might indeed mean that this is the 'Collective Messiah' at work?

Can you imagine the effort necessary to unite the world? It seems improbable.

Surely we could not be so pompous or presumptuous as to believe that we can do it 'alone.' This is what happens more often than not because we cannot get our ego attachment to agenda or identity out of the way. We start wars with others that don't seem to 'get it.'

True humility is to serve the people without attachment to outcome, being guided by the simple nature of addressing what shows up right in front of you/us. It's personal that way.

Once harmony is found in your immediate surroundings, then greater opportunities are presented by those who guide us all from places we may not even be aware of yet; other relatives of cosmic consciousness. This is the place of experiencing the magic of a personal relationship with your 'higher power' or whatever you may choose to call IT.

Do we exercise sound mind and heart? Do we recognize that polarizing to any ID... whether it be Jesus or Lucifer (most prevalent duality)... still separates. Balance is the key to rising above duality consciousness. Many are claiming to embody either, even sometimes both, yet they still are unable to remove the mask to reveal their own individual identity, choosing to identify with an archetypal image rather than their own Divine Nature.

We might call this the Cosmic Conundrum: Who Am I? How do we find, accept, and then live our own individual Path connected to the ONE? Many are frightened that they will lose their identity in the process instead of gaining it.

It is one thing to be self-initiated, the Path where many are called and few choose. It is quite another to claim to BE the ONE, as in the case of many professing to be the return of Einstein, Jesus, Mary, Lucifer, Isis, St. Germain, or whomever. It would seem we have a spiritual epidemic of polyphrenia, many personalities, in reverse.

How could that really be possible?

Indeed something is happening.... just what? Why would one identity incarnate so many times AT

The Messy Antic Complex

THE SAME TIME? Seems a bit confusing, eh? Obviously something is being missed in the process when such confusion exists. How does it all fit together without so much distortion?

The point of wisdom might be to recognize that when one attaches identity to themselves, especially in self-proclaiming ways, then the likelihood of the 'reality' is probably miniscule. You don't have to speak it – others will.

Only by continuing to release attachment to 'identity' can one truly find their perfect path, free of the continued subtle efforts of the ego, desiring to be in control, polarizing paradigm.

Truly… there is NO EGO without WEGO in the current best practices of Spiritual Evolution.

A true spiritual master claims no ownership of the Divine identity flowing through them. They allow the process without attachment to outcome, giving freely their concepts, ideas, heart, mind, spirit, soul and wisdom. As humans, it is rare that we are able to live in such an awareness and reflection of the Divine within us and through us.

The Collective Messiah, the Cosmic Consciousness prevailing in many 'world servers' now is an example of the progress toward true ONENESS. Each has a gift, just as important as the next. It is not the size of the gift, or the manner in which it is delivered. It is important to use it, period.

The fact that it is used that is important. May we all find that ONE in our hearts and share it with the Many who are also here on the planet now.

The only way that we can truly exemplify the Christ Consciousness that we so profess is by leading by example just as Jesus did, or so we believe, by letting go and offering ourselves to the Divine Flow that courses through ALL THAT IS.

Now we might make the distinction here of not following Christianity, but being Christ-like. That is a huge difference.

To fool ourselves into believing that we are separate from anything is another false belief, yet the polarity paradigm seems to edify it still. How do we get beyond this? How about recognizing that all things are available to those that believe? Believe in what?

LOVE... Limitless Oscillating Vibrational Energy. Energy is active and so we must BE active. We are far more advanced technologically than in the times of Jesus, and yet the WORD is still in our HEARTS *and* the KINGDOM OF GOD IS WITHIN.

What we seek to do now is to make the WITHIN, WITHOUT... into the world as we know it. Jesus said to 'Love thine Enemy.' Self-judgment is one of

The Messy Antic Complex

those enemies, among others, self-deprecation at its finest. Imagine what our thoughts do to our bodies.

Maybe, just maybe, we need to learn to love our own 'evil' first. When we can love the worst in ourselves and others, then we can begin to address these features in positive ways, resolving and rehabilitating rather than resisting their obvious existence. Awareness, recognition, change…

This WORK takes nothing short of ultimate cooperation and collaboration from the depths of our Souls, with natural/divine order. We each have gifts as well as skill sets we've garnered from our living in this world.

Would it not make sense to honor these both, bridging our inner and outer worlds now?

Only when we do this individually can we do it collectively, sharing our wealth and our wisdom, through demonstrating how to work together for the greater good of all, including self and others.

Attachments to identity or ownership of ideas only get in the way of this process of progress toward a new world order of harmony among people and planet. Finding solace in the Heart of Creation comes from forgiveness of self, others, and situations that have not met our expectations for whatever reason.

Even the most advanced souls still have expectations and they are constantly vigilant of the need to detach and forgive. Forgiveness is powerful, both for self and others as we let go of expectations that weren't met.

So what about giving our enemies food, clothing and shelter as part of our planetary evolution? That is Christ-like.

There is a natural order of movement within this Collective Messiah as we each bring our offerings, our willingness, to give to the whole. Many are experiencing delays in what they feel are important projects for them, and the world, yet they refuse to relinquish 'control' of their ideas and how they are to be implemented.

Wouldn't it make sense to combine all ideas, as the natural process would synergize them into a greater potential for actual manifestation?

Sadly, this is a lesson it seems we are still learning. Could we actually choose to bring all our talents and skills together and WILLINGLY SHARE them?

Do you think that you, personally, would be willing to offer your most vulnerable secrets for the benefit of the entire world?

Believing that there are secrets might be your first step in an undesirable direction. There are no secrets

The Messy Antic Complex

when you reach this level of awareness. This does not mean that we 'know everything' yet instantaneous answers to pertinent questions occur often. Remember to, 'ask, seek and knock.'

In reality whatever we choose, the polardigm {polarity paradigm} leads us hOMe. From the place of extremes, we can recognize all the paths of the polardigm and how they benefit us all to learn the ways of LOVE.

As a Zen master once said, "There is interaction if there is a call for it, no interaction if there is no call for it." It would seem that the Universe is calling for it now as we enter the new millennium. Faith, trust and allowance in this new living awareness *is* the Way, the ultimate showing of strength on the Path.

We begin to gather together now in celebration of our birthright, understanding that we are all part of the ONE, each with our personal path that compliments the whole. Knowing is showing. Showing is caring. Caring is giving. Giving is receiving. Receiving is limitless love pouring through our minds, hearts and bodies toward joining in the ONE.

As each of our masks is revealed in our discovery process, we allow the ONE to play through our actions in the ultimate play of life, love and happiness for all. Could it be that, "All things are possible to those who believe?"

Imagine the possibilities.

What if many believed in a new world order of harmony among people and planet? Imagine the shift in consciousness it would take to facilitate the demonstration of that belief. We might notice a proliferation of self-awareness gurus, motivational books and movies, non-profit service organizations or a nation electing change. It's a start.

The thing is, if Jesus were to have an influence on us now in preparation for his return, wouldn't He expect us to have learned how to live together? That was one of his key points, to love one another. I'm just thinking that if/when he does show up we ought to have done the prep work as dictated by the Word in our hearts.

Now I want to make sure that you don't think I'm proselytizing here. I don't think Christianity is any better than any other religion. As a matter of fact, I think they all compete instead of collaborate and cooperate. None is better or worse, except for how their devotees behave toward one another.

We need to look for what brings us together, not what keeps us separate. Unless and until we learn that, our world will remain in turmoil.

My hopes are that you received something valuable about your life and living it to its fullest by reading this book. My dreams are that you will become part of the solution and we can all work as ONE someday. It is a natural progression of evolution.

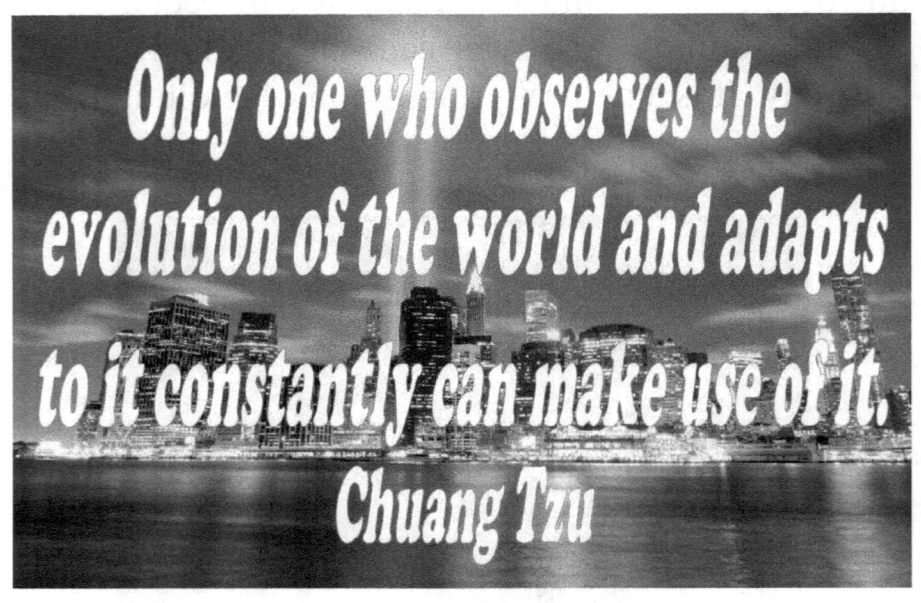

Let no one think that he has learned all, because there is no ending to learning.

Sri Swami Satchidananda

How About Transition?

Across the Web and in our communities there are so many versions of how this group or that group is vying for position to lead the way to the New World Order, some as cabals and pundits and others as world servers and stewards.

How to we work together?

Just the mention of the phrase 'New World Order' carries so many different 'charges' of emotional bindings that it is hard to find the 'truth' to it all.

What were your thoughts when you read the phrase?

Do you see how sensitized we can become from marginalized information and the projections of others, however well-intended?

What if this is just a process?

We know, or at least some have a sense, that all things are connected – a holistic model of consciousness permeates creation. Quantum sciences are pointing toward this as fact now. We still choose to separate ourselves from others today, though. It happens everywhere.

What are the main challenges?

Fear is being promoted at the very top of national leadership across the world. Even when prompted to contact or communicate with another, our 'logic' often prohibits the interaction due to fear of misunderstanding, rejection or threat of appearing less than what we think we should. We are insecure.

Can we affect change where primary belief systems seem diametrically opposed?

Can we offer a solution?

Do we really want solutions?

It has taken us centuries to arrive at the present conditions. Can or will it change in a few years?

Will we rise above fear and embrace a new way, a new living awareness of harmony in the world?

How can we open our minds to understand something we've never experienced?

What if we were able to acknowledge the obvious?

Our minds and hearts are still in opposition. We fear what we do not know or have not experienced. It seems counter-intuitive at best.

Oftentimes a new experience brings such a 'rush' of energy that we confuse it as a threat rather than a thread in the fabric of our evolution. We lock up – the fight or flight syndrome so common in psychology. I like the 'butt-pucker effect.'

Are these our only choices?

Do we have another choice yet unexplored?

How About Transition?

We can rise in consciousness but we generally take the mandatory rollercoaster ride to get there. It is our unconscious patterned desire for continued separation that inhibits our ability to connect, a pattern so deep and in such conflict with self/Self that wars are fought across the planet because of it.

Ancient Mayan and even Sanskrit terms in use today indicate we might want to consider some alternatives. 'In lakesh' (I am another you) and 'Namasté' (internal and external obeisance to thee) both acknowledge the oneness in self and others. Whose eyes are we using?

The humble bow of recognition that is part of many cultures moves us closer toward a sense of unity, or at least understanding. It is more than respect. I am challenged to see and sense myself in another, even with the extensive experience and knowing of this truth and an attitude of gratitude.

What about those completely unaware of self?

The Internet brings us closer in communication and yet further apart from physical communion with others. What do we really want anyway?

The hot new belief system says we can attract what we want by identifying what we desire, giving it attention, and allowing it to happen.

Easier said than done, yet it warrants further consideration for sure. Implementing an action plan that creates the magnet for the desire to manifest is the key that we seem to ignore, thinking that we can defy known scientific rules: potential energy remains at rest until acted upon. So let's apply the science of creating.

Conversely it is an obvious strain in feeling and logic to eliminate the concept of identifying what we don't want in order to move closer to what we do. Still the objective is to create, co-create or construct new thoughtforms of a stronger magnetism that allows matter and spirit to coalesce in accordance with this new living awareness.

I've heard it called 'structural tension' as an element in the creative process. How do we make the process simple?

Simplicity of being, doing and having is the goal for all spiritual seekers, allowing the greater consciousness to permeate their worlds and guide their daily movements. Simple gratification and validation is also the goal of most individuals in daily living, unconsciously desiring to love and be loved in the spirit of oneness.

We talk a good line, but the result is tainted with pushing or pulling energy to move as many mountains as possible with as little effort as we can muster. We really look for the easy route.

This is not to say that humans are lazy, yet they do tend to avoid the stretch to actually make things simple in their daily lives, let alone shift into a heart-centered awareness. Once a heart-centered awareness is achieved, though, the knowing moves us toward more prudent paths.

Our perceived intelligence often convinces us not to listen to the still small voice within, even after a so-called 'spiritual awakening.' We rarely challenge the notion of duality, yet it is the stumbling block laid before us in our quest to find balance and harmony.

Even science and religion strive to find harmony in their expressions of reality and thousands of books have been written on the subject of Unity… unified field theory to universal love, M Theory to The Masters of the Far East and much more.

How can we simplify the understanding to make it practical enough to implement daily?

Would it be easier to simply look at the existing systems in our global economy, for instance, and focus on developing life-friendly processes and protocols? Perhaps.

How can we better manage our resources, both human and material, while promoting a sense of unification without subjugation?

We are faced with choices on a moment to moment basis, pushed and pulled by this or that to make a decision about our lives, great or small. Granted, some do not want to choose; they simply want to follow or be told what to do so they do not have to be accountable or responsible for their actions.

It is far easier a path to be led than to lead. It is a challenge to think, let alone change.

It's interesting how the two words are only three letters different. The momentum in the world of challenge is often fear driven, through liabilities, limitations and excuses. We must make the changes necessary in our individual worlds first – the rest will take care of itself.

Is there a collective voice somewhere that guides our quest in this urge to merge with the Divine?

Can we change liability to liberality, limitation to luminary or excuse to executor?

One would hope.

Symbolically Speaking

It is quite revealing that a cross-section of our DNA helix viewed in black and white (light pulsing on and off) looks quite similar to the yin/yang symbol.

Could this be a sign placed for our recognition, similar to the primer in the movie 'Contact'? The yin/yang resembles the on/off top-down view of a DNA helix.

We have the key to creating a union between homo and sapiens, right here on Earth. Could another similar sign, the '666,' denote a scientific union... the number of man... carbon? We have all condensed into physical form to be here now, as consciousness in a body.

Yet today in many metaphysical gatherings, the 'Ascension' is probably the most present notion of the new millennium and the projected result of the alignment with the Galactic Center in 2012.

What does that mean?

To them [2012ers] we rise out of 3rd dimensional reality – duality of war and peace and experience a new world order of harmony among people and planet. Perhaps that is possible?

There is a transition from 3D to 4D or 5D, but the picture gets hazy there. No concrete description is offered and many believe there will even be two

Earths; one that remains for those not willing to 'ascend' and one that is now inhabited by those who have ascended. Did I mention this before? Google: Multi-Plane Awareness.

Do you see a bit of the dualistic framework remaining in that scenario? How would the view from ONE appear?

Perceptively, our heart beat shifts for a poignant realization as we drop anchor in consciousness, a noticeably stronger pulse that attracts our attention for a moment. Is it possible that an imminent burst of energy from Source or some kind of cosmic ray gun will wipe the heart-drive of incongruent belief systems? Again, one can hope.

Our movement through space into the Photon Belt precipitates a subtle rise in vibration, evidenced by a rise in the cycles per second pulse of our planet, an increase of a nearly imperceptible degree in human experience. Or are we being duped?

The Schumann Resonance measures the remaining 'buzz' after a lightning strike, which gives an indication of the change in the Earth's pulse. Although there are many who reference this 'data' as changing, in fact it hasn't at all.

Most humans seem to be oblivious; others sense an impending cosmic shift toward an age of

Symbolically Speaking

enlightenment. Is there a cosmic change agent with their fingers on the volume control?

Or, are there many on the WAN?

What about the various belief systems that have at their core a need to have good and evil? Is this truly a Divine characteristic or simply ignorant humans projecting their own circumstance on a divine framework so it 'fits' their mold.

Modern theologians seem to breeze by the knowledge that 'satan' came from the Greek 'thetan' and means 'thinker.'

As I recall, the word for 'fallen' was more like 'condensed' but the minds of the translators weren't able to understand the concept at the time. It would seem 'logical' that cosmic intelligence would learn how to condense into physical form through their evolutionary process.

Could we call that 'descending' mortals?

It would also seem that the 'universe' seeks to replicate itself in finite forms, creating further diversity and universal order ascending from chaos. We already know the process of natural law, a movement from chaos to order.

The number of man (666) turns out to be the number of protons, electrons and neutrons in the carbon atom, the basis for all organic life forms, including humans. We sure have become the Beast.

How about that?

In spite of religious reluctance we are moving out of the fear, guilt and shame game and into a more holistic model. Is it too simple to believe that Lucifer (angel of light and music, by the way) was asked to take the lead in the process, being the Most High and all? What a fall that must've been.

In spite of your resistance to that thought, wouldn't it make sense if you were picking someone that was going to experience all the hatred and judgment from humans unwilling to accept their own responsibility for their actions?

Why do we project our own problems and evilness on such a being?

Do we ever take responsibility?

Is it so hard for humans to admit their own thoughts and actions are incongruent with their professed beliefs in an unconditional loving creator?

Don't forget that our translated version omits that 'creators' or 'Gods' was indeed plural in the beginning. No mention of Lilith, either.

Omnipresent, omniscient and omnipotent lends itself to the trinity constructs. The Nag Hamadi presents the one intelligence of creation as three

Symbolically Speaking

expressions or manifestations as I recall. Nearly every religion has an expression of a trinity.

Heck, the proton, electron and neutron make up all physical material and with one exception (hydrogen) any kind of intelligent design has to be present in the material constructs. I thought about that one a long, long time.

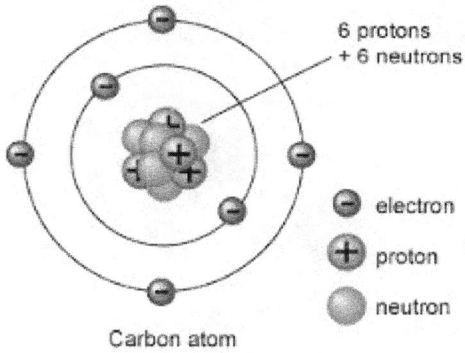

Carbon atom

The GOD Participle.... BEing

another view of the Higgs-boson, formerly known as the GOD Particle.

I'd like to finish this little excursion with a trip into quantum physics. It apparently is a very challenging subject area with equations and theories on the constructs, dimensions and layers of reality. I hope to express things in a more simple fashion, yet there is some complexity that cannot be avoided.

The GOD Participle? What the heck is that? I'll get to that in a moment, but I want to keep you guessing for now. Meanwhile, I'd like to take a look at the infamous 'GOD Particle'... Higgs-boson as it is known. I'm asking you to join me in an exploration of another perspective of possibility that is perhaps way outside the box.

First of all, let's look at what the Higgs-boson is reported to represent. Let's look at a few definitions from across the web. From the Free Dictionary:

> A hypothetical, massive subatomic particle with zero electric charge. The Higgs boson is postulated to interact with other particles in such a way as to impart mass to them. It is predicted by the standard model, but has yet to be isolated experimentally. The Higgs boson is named after its discoverer, British theoretical physicist Peter Ware Higgs (born 1929).

Here's another interesting take from the Science - How It Works site:

> Can't matter just inherently have mass without the Higgs-boson confusing things? Not according to the standard model. But physicists have found a solution. What if all particles have no inherent mass, but instead gain mass by passing through a field? This field, known as a Higgs field, could affect different particles in different ways. Photons could slide through unaffected, while W and Z bosons would get bogged down with mass. In fact, assuming the Higgs-boson exists, everything that has mass gets it by interacting with the all-powerful Higgs field, which occupies the entire universe. Like the other fields covered by the standard model, the Higgs one would need a carrier particle to affect other particles, and that particle is known as the Higgs boson.

Now, that might give you at least a partial working knowledge of what the excitement is all about for the 'discovery' of the particle. Here's the really interesting twist, though... There was no particle, but the 'decay' of which was determined to reveal the existence of the particle even though it was never 'seen.' I personally find the whole quantum physics

The GOD Participle...

perspective a little far-fetched. Science is supposed to be about hard facts and repeatable results.

I'm fairly intelligent and it's hard for me to wrap my head around a field yielding a particle that transmits mass to other particles. Maybe I'm just not smart enough to be able to understand the process.

It reminds me of the discoveries at Los Alamos that revealed the scientists observing experiments actually had an effect on them. So thought seems to affect the process, but doesn't necessarily carry mass with it, unless it's just baggage from a belief system.

At any rate, it just seems counter-intuitive that matter or mass is transferred via some theoretical particle. Furthermore, it would seem even more preposterous that an explosion would produce any such particle.

That explosion was the result of ramming two protons together at near-light speed. These 'hadrons' theoretically fuse together when collided and form another even smaller particle, a remnant. It's like slamming two oranges together at breakneck speeds and having a fused seed as a result.

That really makes a lot of sense, doesn't it?

Perhaps it does. With all the technical jargon and mathematical equations, the analogy gets lost in the intellectual vocabulary that only scientists supposedly understand.

Okay, so now that we've made some progress regarding the 'understanding' of the Higgs-boson perhaps there is another explanation or even discovery that has gone unnoticed by the scientific community. It would seem that the lenses from which they are looking might be a little skewed or undervalued by 'what' they are look for instead of acknowledging what is really being 'seen' from simple observation. The discovery is just as magnificent, but may come as quite a surprise if they are willing to look.

Of course I could be totally wrong, but I think the logic will hold up at least for the purpose of sharing another possibility. Let's start with just the observation of the explosion. It is at a sub-atomic level that is so small we need huge instruments just to be able to measure it.

In the electromagnetic spectrum and according to M-Theory, there are multiple dimensions or layers of 'reality' as one might perceive. The notion seems to be consistent with all the layers of bandwidth and understanding of the various frequencies that have been associated with different types of 'rays' whether from a scientific point of view or from an 'ascended master' POV. The latter involved varies

The GOD Participle...

'rays' of consciousness instead of electromagnetic notations. Both probably describe the same thing.

So, this explosion then may produce a rip in the fabric between said 'dimensions' or 'rays' that is observable as the 'decay' of the particle in question rather than indicating an actual particle. The 'decay' is perhaps the reverse or 'repair' of the rip instead.

Rather than proving the 'particle' theory it may indeed prove that M-Theory is indeed true and yet unseen in this example because the eyes that were looking had a different spectacle in mind. Like I said, it may not be true. However, I think it at least is worthy of some further consideration.

Alright, I mentioned the GOD Participle earlier in reference to the discovery. (I just have to share that there has been an appearance of a hummingbird several times outside my window as I've been writing this, peering in on me as it were.)

What is the GOD Participle? If you are an educator, especially an English teacher, then you'll remember the definition of a participle:

> a word formed from a verb (e.g., going, gone, being, been) and used as an adjective (e.g., working woman, burned toast) or a noun (e.g., good breeding). In English, participles are also used to make compound verb forms (e.g., is going, has been).

The definition gives away the answer. It's quite simply the most elegant word in the English language, too. In order to observe the process of how I came up with the perspective that allowed me to present an alternative view of the Higgs-boson notion I had to be in a particular place.

In the presentation of this place across a plethora of fields it is simply known as.... BEing. That is the GOD Participle. Perhaps you can explore it further on your own. I encourage that strongly.

Like the separation of people that religion promotes, scientific perspectives are no different. It would be amazing to witness great minds step back and consider the possibilities their discoveries may indeed provide for mankind's evolution toward harmony among people and planet.

Science and spirituality seem to be on the same page in regard to the layers of bandwidth across the electromagnetic spectrum and the multiple dimensions of consciousness that we have barely scratched the surface in understanding, let alone garnering the wisdom it presents.

We can only see a minute percentage of the visible light across the electromagnetic spectrum. Here's some information I found regarding the scientific calculation of just how much we can see:

The GOD Participle...

Let's examine the available information. The electromagnetic spectrum is usually considered to extend from radio waves to gamma rays, with frequencies from about 10000 Hz to 10^{19} Hz, respectively, while visible light goes from red to violet with frequencies from about 4×10^{14} Hz to about 7.5×10^{14} Hz, respectively.

So, if the entire spectrum is taken to span 15 orders of magnitude ($\log_{10}(10^{19}) = 19$, $\log_{10}(10^4) = 4$, and $19 - 4 = 15$) while the visible spectrum spans only 0.35 of an order of magnitude, then we can say that the visible spectrum is $100\% \times 0.35/15$ of the entire electromagnetic spectrum, which works out to about 2.3%.

But that is on a logarithmic scale, so let's do the calculation again on a linear scale:

The entire spectrum has the range 10^{19} Hz - 10^4 Hz, which is $0.999999999999999 \times 10^{19}$ Hz. The visible spectrum has the range 3.5×10^{14} Hz.

147

100%*3.5x1014/0.999999999999999x1019 = 0.0035%.

So, on a logarithmic scale of frequency, visible light is 2.3% of the whole electromagnetic spectrum, while on a linear scale it is 0.0035%.

If you would rather do the calculation using wavelengths I think there is enough information here for you to able to do so.

John Link, MadSci Physicist

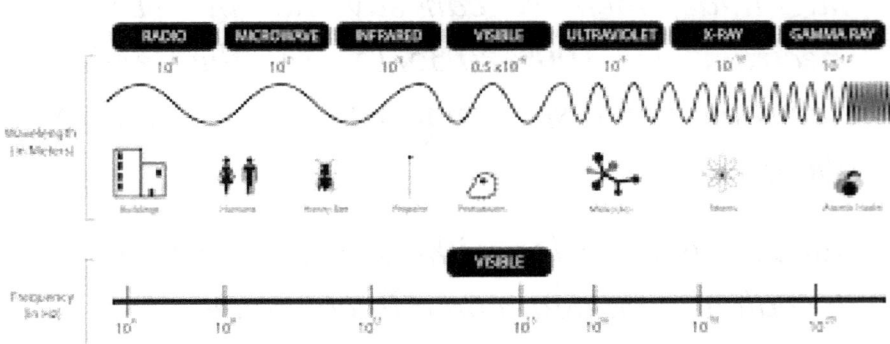

The GOD Participle…

I'll finish by quoting a current-day wise man, or at least some think so, regarding our ability to call forth into the darkness in making sense common.

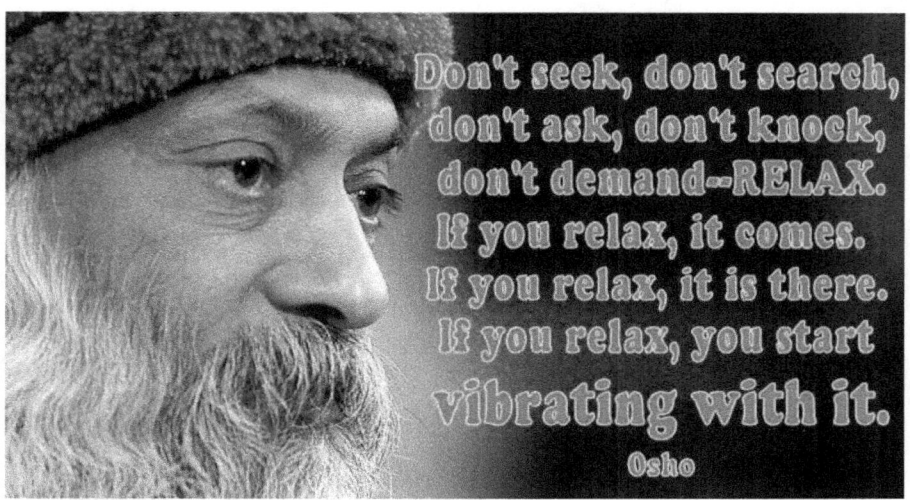

Thanks allowing me to rent space in your head for bit. I hope you found value in the duration of our shared space.

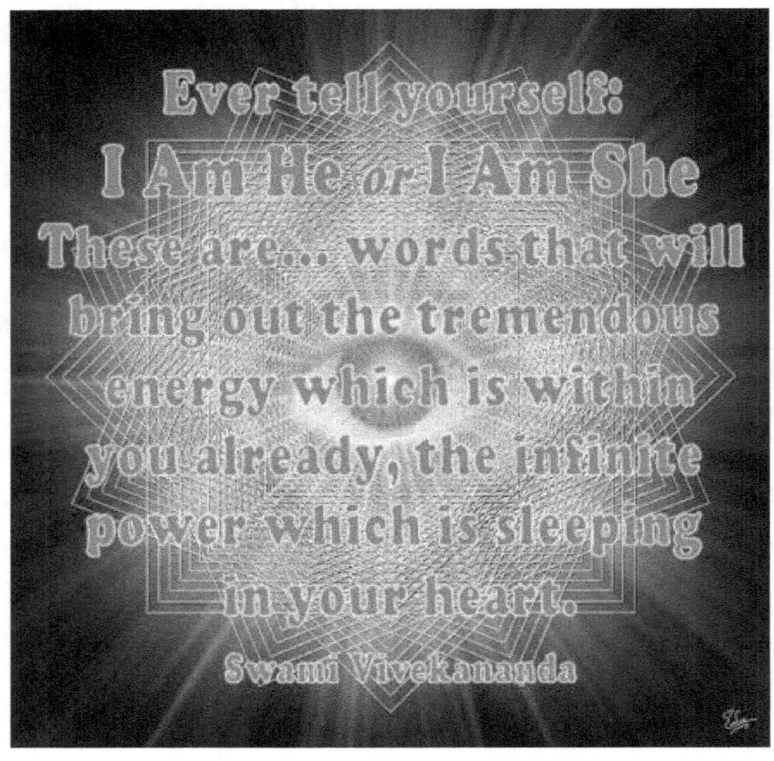

Soular Revolution

There is a point of light within each human being that is connected to the Great Light. This is an awareness within the teachings of all major religions, yet has no religious affiliation. Most refer to this as our soul, eternal and immutable, though we continue to act our of character with it. Science is now revealing that this condition exists, though it doesn't tell us how to actualize our true nature.

If we were to consider what our true nature is in its purest form, what might that be? Living in harmony with creation? We certainly have not been doing that, yet. We have a chance to move beyond past pains, unfulfilled and unspoken expectations and even social distancing that we've been doing long before our recent pandemic.

If you had the chance to live more fully and enjoy the life you were meant to live, would you be willing to give up any and/or all distractions for it to happen in your lifetime?

Of course the first impression is probably one of a religious nature, like some kind of prophetic fulfillment. Indeed it might be, though it still lacks definition and impact on individuals within whatever belief system may be applied and goes further to unite them all at a very simplistic level.

They all mention the ONE in the Many in some form, but how does that really show up in a practical application? How do we engage it?

So let's start with an assumption – each human on earth has an essence within them that we call a life force or soul. The further assumption of where we come from and where we go is described as a Great Light of inclusion, before and after our lives on Earth. That appears to be a ubiquitous postulate throughout all religions, which gives us a solid foundation from which to grow together in a new way that unites rather than divides.

Now the obvious counter with atheists is there is no Great Light. Recent scientific discoveries in quantum mechanics show that there is a greater reality, multiple dimensions that contain a consciousness, still lacking definition that is tethered across space and time. Quantum entanglement, spooky action at a distance, is described as two photons vibrating at the same rate at a distance from each other. There is a resonance between the two, comparable to the resonance of energy of individuals with similar life paths that eventually interact at their appointed time.

Necessary Assumptions

Let's assume there are perfect reflections of that psycho-spiritual science contained in the notion that each of us has a point of light (figuratively and literally) within us that is a fragment or individuation of the Great Light that is connected to the physical form and animates it exquisitely. The combination is a magnificent creation we still have yet to fully understand, though we are making headway as we seek to discover our perfected form, fit and function in the world – what most call our 'purpose' in life.

Seeking purpose has been a enigma throughout human existence. From research and study of those who believe they've found purpose, it seems to begin with subtle impressions, a kind of intuitive notion of the direction one needs to take. Many refer to it as a 'calling' in simple terms.

Over time, they begin to recognize more definitive signs through 'coincidence' or more properly termed, 'synchronicity.' Synchronicity is defined as: *the simultaneous occurrence of events which appear significantly related but have no discernible causal connection.* It's the magic of life.

Now we need to make another assumption, perhaps a leap of faith or trust. We've been informed through the ages that there is One that operates in us all. The efficacy and integration of the many (human inhabitants of Earth) into the One calls for a sublime weaving of the skill sets among those who were initially 'called' into their given professions into a performing art, a tapestry of life if you will, that has at its core an understanding of structure and uniformity of purpose. Given what we already know, it isn't difficult to imagine this kind of structural integrity embedded in the genetic material we all carry.

How do we access that genetic code or even the cursory understanding of our individual purpose and a visceral experience of it? Could it be an aspect of soul, the point of light within us connected to the Great Light, performing at a new level and perhaps even a global scale. Is the ability we have of focusing attention, intention and action toward acquiescing to this inner understanding such a leap of logic? It's sure different than the intellectual approach yet fits the Scientific Model. We can explore the hypothesis and observe the results, often so subtle we might miss it if we weren't paying attention. The results are there nevertheless. The process is repeatable and with consistent results.

Many have spent their lives exploring the nature of our being, doing and having as it relates to a greater framework or reality beyond the subjective. The bridge between the subjective and objective occurs by the correlation of data, experience and interpretation, serving to distill a kind of ubiquitous understanding beyond the individual languages.

Many explain the same process using their own terms, though the cross-referencing has only been in intellectualized discussions of the bridge between science and spirituality.

Free Will or Destiny?

Is the call for a Soular Revolution a personal choice using our free will? Perhaps, though as with the 'calling' toward a certain lifestyle, profession or vocation, it may preclude free will to a certain degree. It comes from a much deeper place in our being; that inner truth looking place that after all the attempts to quiet or silence it, it remains unscathed from attack. It is a place many refer to as unconditional love, though it transcends our understanding of it yet. That place of unconditional love is free of fear and rejection, so there are no barriers to garnering pure information.

We've developed filters throughout the ages, ones that protect and serve our individual needs, but we've also found those same filters have produced a dystopian society that is too often afraid of itself and produces threats to keep us afraid, angry, ignorant and immobile. It takes courage to let go of the life we think we have in order to gain a new and better one that serves all, as well as individual needs, as a collaborative organism. The rise toward a Type I Civilization is such a path.

Speaking of filters, there is one that instills dread and fear in humanity – the perception that a system such as described above takes away personal freedoms and rights in some kind of a command and control environment where people can't buy or sell without being a member. Many believe this to be a fulfillment of prophecy, especially with the point of view that history repeats itself and the rise and fall of civilizations will continue as a result. Remember we do have free will, the choice to be different, to ascend from old belief systems and rise to a new order of thinking.

This new order of thinking is inclusive, just like the Great Light. No one is left behind, except by their own choice, and humanity is served through the development and application of new technologies that work with natural resources and our planetary energy as a symbiotic process that supports life and sustainability. So far we have not understood just how fragile our symbiotic lives are, missing the notion that we *can* have harmony among people and planet. In fact, it is a natural progression of our evolution, linking soul and sustainability.

A Shift of Ages

In another view, the process of moving from one age to another gives us a larger view of change, from the Piscean to the Aquarian Age. So many ancient calendars foretell of such a change, where chaos ensues first as the old paradigms are shattered. It doesn't matter how as we can cite so many references in our current conundrum. The fact is we are moving into a higher order of activity as a civilization and planet, fueled by cosmic influences we are just beginning to understand. So many authors, explorers, scientists et al have produced so much material now available online and offline that edify this reality.

There is a transition period, though, where we have to face our deepest fears and resolve them individually and collectively. This, too, is a process happening simultaneously with the events and situations occurring locally, nationally and globally at present. Too often we become distracted with the activity and the narrative of the old paradigm in its last attempts to survive, though its natural decay is in perfect order as well. As any civilization evolves, it leaves old paradigms behind.

Unfortunately for humans who've developed a 'gotta have it now' lifestyle and mindset, this is no easy or fast transition. It is in process, though. Make no mistake. It's hard to see when you are caught in the maelstrom, the chaos of figuring out what you need to do today and tomorrow to keep afloat.

We're all in relation-ships being buffeted on the ocean of emotion, seeking safe harbor on a distant shore we cannot see yet. This is where faith, love and trust is tested to the extreme, yet will prevail because of the embedded activity in a Soular Revolution in the core of our nature.

Challenge to Change:

Love is the driving force of the life within us and all around us, by whatever name you wish to call it, the essence is LOVE. The two things we all want most out of life is to love and be loved, right? It's ubiquitous among humankind. It comes fro the depths of our Being, our SOUL. Whether you believe in that or not, the desire for Love still prevails in the hearts and minds of all creatures on Earth.

How do we create *value* in the 21st Century? How do we create *bridges* for a holistic systems approach to planetary administration and merge diversity effectively? Whether we fear or welcome it, there is a 'new world order' that is emerging. How do we, as planetary citizens, make sure that the momentum takes us toward living as ONE – one people, one planet, one time?

How do we truly LOVE ONE ANOTHER?

Did you notice that 'challenge' and 'change' are only 3 letters different? We took that challenge, converted the LLE to Liabilities, Limitations and Excuses we use to keep us from meeting personal achievements and taking collaborative action toward practical solutions. One of our goals is to remove those very Liabilities, Limitations and Excuses by providing sound leadership direction and purpose.

It all seems to make perfect sense when we realize that there are enough resources to feed, clothe, house and provide health care for everyone. We've placed the economics of war over human life, though, and that mindset has to change soon or we'll self-destruct. The Profit Over People Regime is ending; **People and Planet Over Profit** is emerging now. Even with those supposedly working for 'good'... are they more interested in sharing or selling you something?

The truly confusing piece of information is that we spend more money on corporate and military functions than, if redirected, would provide more than enough funds to feed, clothe, house and care for everyone. Of course those are statistics, but what if they are true? Today we've seen a government attempt to manipulate its public with a 'Stimulus Package' to assuage the financial devastation caused by ill-prepared and/or strategically planned stay-at-home edicts.

Soular Revolution Embraces Practical Solutions

Chaos seems to rule in 2020, yet it holds a perfected vision of our unrealized potential. We all have a place inside of us that is compassionate, even loving toward our fellow human beings and all life on earth. At present (June 2020) America is suffering from insidious surreptitious activity causing our society to fall apart with no great leadership to speak of today.

This awareness is a place of great pain for many as we experience a major transition in our freedoms, leadership positions and our global environment.

Many feel powerless, like their lives mean little to those who are supposed to be their advocates in governmental affairs.

In a larger view, our way of life is being threatened by our lack of participation in the process we've taken for granted as 'good for us.'

This transition foretold long ago is destined to be a transformation of humanity, a revolution of soul long awaited, where people are empowered to act, to speak and to work toward common goals more effectively through the networks and technology that have been developing.

We know the 'systems' are in place to deliver the goods, so to speak; the systems have just had bad management practices from the people in charge to date. It is up to us all to change that now.

The road ahead is full of challenges and chaos, for the time being. The 5Ps of Life are a guide for us all for now – **Patience, Persistence, Perseverance, Passion,** and **Purpose**.

We shall overcome any and all distractions with a style and grace only a higher order of consciousness emerging within us could provide!

Explore Further

Author's Websites

BeTheDream.com - Coaching

BeTheDream.info – Zen's Blog

BeTheDream.net – original website

IndependenceArizona.com - activism

PlanetaryCitizens.net – community

PlanckMedia.com – digital agency

TeamPartnering.com - facilitation

ZenBenefiel.com – a collection

Amazon.com/author/zendor – Author's page

About the Author

Bruce Lee Benefiel was orphaned at birth and adopted at 6 weeks old, his biological history still a mystery. His search for roots revealed the adoption records, stored by the State, were destroyed in a flood and the Department of Health only had non-identifying information in their files. It provides for much speculation.

"It's tough for most people to relate to the depths of curiosity and discovery of one who knows no terrestrial heritage and apparently is open to worlds beyond the scope of even good script writers," he's been heard to say.

He began having OBEs and extraterrestrial 'contactee' experiences, among others, long before his 10th birthday. A gifted athlete, empath and stellar student, he claims that being an 'eduholic' with an addiction to knowing truth that leads one to explore the unknown repeatedly as a part of living.

With two Master's degrees in Business and various successes in aerospace, education and special events as accomplishments, 'Zen' (as he is known now) enjoys his work as a 'Possibilities Coagulator' helping others put people, places and things into a executable framework for achieving dreams and goals, complete with action and/or business plan.

His primary business is quite aptly named… BE The Dream, LLC, coaching and consulting entrepreneurs, startup and small businesses. He also facilitates road and bridge 'partnering' pre-construction workshops for various contractors, DOTs and the Federal Highways Administration under Team Partnering, LLC.

Notes

www.ingramcontent.com/pod-product-compliance
Lightning Source LLC
Chambersburg PA
CBHW061945070426
42450CB00007BA/1057